ALL OF IT SINGING

BOOKS BY LINDA GREGG

Too Bright to See
Alma
The Sacraments of Desire
Chosen by the Lion
Things and Flesh
In the Middle Distance

ALL OF IT SINGING
New and Selected Poems

Linda Gregg

Graywolf Press

Too Bright to See was originally published by Graywolf Press in 1981. *Alma* was originally published by Random House in 1985. *Too Bright to See* and *Alma* were reissued together and published by Graywolf Press in 2002. *The Sacraments of Desire* was originally published by Graywolf Press in 1991. *Chosen by the Lion* was originally published by Graywolf Press in 1994. *Things and Flesh* was originally published by Graywolf Press in 1999. *In the Middle Distance* was originally published by Graywolf Press in 2006.

This publication is made possible by funding provided in part by a grant from the Minnesota State Arts Board, through an appropriation by the Minnesota State Legislature, a grant from the National Endowment for the Arts, and private funders. Significant support has also been provided by Target; the McKnight Foundation; and other generous contributions from foundations, corporations, and individuals. To these organizations and individuals we offer our heartfelt thanks.

This book is made possible through a partnership with the College of Saint Benedict, and honors the legacy of S. Mariella Gable, a distinguished teacher at the College. Support has been provided by the Lee and Rose Warner Foundation as part of the Warner Reading Program.

A Jane Kenyon book, funded in part by the Estate of Jane Kenyon to support the ongoing careers of women poems published by Graywolf Press.

Published by Graywolf Press
250 Third Avenue North, Suite 600
Minneapolis, Minnesota 55401

www.graywolfpress.org

Published in the United States of America

ISBN 978-1-55597-507-4 (cloth)
ISBN 978-1-55597-578-4 (paper)

4 6 8 9 7 5 3

Library of Congress Control Number: 2010937516

Cover design: Kyle G. Hunter

Cover art: Fresco from Akrotiri, Thera (Santorini). Aegean, c. 1650 BCE. National Archaeological Museum, Athens, Greece. Photo credit: Scala/Art Resource, NY.

CONTENTS

from *Alma*

from *The Sacraments of Desire*

from *Chosen by the Lion*

from *Things and Flesh*

from *In the Middle Distance*

New Poems

For *Jack Gilbert*

IT WAS LIKE BEING ALIVE TWICE

from *Too Bright to See*

WE MANAGE MOST WHEN
WE MANAGE SMALL

What things are steadfast? Not the birds.
Not the bride and groom who hurry
in their brevity to reach one another.
The stars do not blow away as we do.
The heavenly things ignite and freeze.
But not as my hair falls before you.
Fragile and momentary, we continue.
Fearing madness in all things huge
and their requiring. Managing as thin light
on water. Managing only greetings
and farewells. We love a little, as the mice
huddle, as the goat leans against my hand.
As the lovers quickening, riding time.
Making safety in the moment. This touching
home goes far. This fishing in the air.

THE GIRL I CALL ALMA

The girl I call Alma who is so white
is good, isn't she? Even though she does not speak,
you can tell by her distress that she is
just like the beach and the sea, isn't she?
And she is disappearing, isn't that good?
And the white curtains, and the secret smile
are just her way with the lies, aren't they?
And that we are not alone, ever.
And that everything is backwards
otherwise.
And that inside the no is the yes. Isn't it?
Isn't it? And that she is the god who perishes:
the food we eat, the body we fuck,
the loose net we throw out that gathers her.
Fish! Fish! White sun! Tell me we are one
and that it's the others who scar me,
not you.

THE CHORUS SPEAKS HER WORDS
AS SHE DANCES

You are perishing like the old men. Already your arms are gone,
your legs filled with scented straw tied off at the knees.
Your hair hacked off. How I wish I could take on each part
of you as it leaves. Sweet mouse princess, I would sing
like a nightingale, higher and higher to a screech
which the heart recognizes, which the helpless stars enjoy—
like the sound of the edge of grass.

I adore you. I take you seriously, even if I am alone in this.
If you had arms, you would lift them up I know. Ah, Love,
what knows that?

(How tired and barren I am.)
Mouse eyes. Lady with white on her face. What will the world do
without you? What will the sea do?
How will they remember the almond flowers? And the old man,
smiling, holding up the new lamb: whom will he hold it up to?
What will the rough men do after their rounds of drinks
and each one has told his story? How will they get home
without the sound of the shore anymore?

(I think my doll is the sole survivor, my Buddha mouse, moon
princess, amputee who still has the same eyes.
With her song that the deer sings when it is terrified.
That the rabbits sing, grass sings, fish, the sea sings:
a sound like frost, like sleet, high keening, shrill squeak.
Zo-on-na, Kannon, I hold each side of her deeply affected face
and turn on the floor.

This song comes from the bottom of the hill at night, in summer.
From a distance as fine as that first light on those islands.
As the lights on the dark island which held still while our ship
came away. This is the love song that lasts through history.
I am a joke and a secret here, and I will leave.
It is morning now. The light whitens her face more than ever.)

There She Is

When I go into the garden, there she is.
The specter holds up her arms to show
that her hands are eaten off.
She is silent because of the agony.
There is blood on her face.
I can see she has done this to herself.
So she would not feel the other pain.
And it is true, she does not feel it.
She does not even see me.
It is not she anymore, but the pain itself
that moves her. I look and think
how to forget. How can I live while she
stands there? And if I take her life
what will that make of me? I cannot
touch her, make her conscious.
It would hurt her too much.
I hear the sound all through the air
that was her eating, but it is on its own now,
completely separate from her. I think
I am supposed to look. I am not supposed
to turn away. I am supposed to see each detail
and all expression gone. My God, I think,
if paradise is to be here
it will have to include her.

THE BECKETT KIT

I finally found a way of using the tree.
If the man is lying down with the sheep
while the dog stands, then the wooden tree
can also stand, in the back, next to the dog.

They show their widest parts
(the dog sideways, the tree frontal)
so that being next to each other
they function as a landscape.

I tried for nearly two months to use the tree.
I tried by putting the man,
standing of course, very far from the sheep
but in more or less the same plane.
At one point I had him almost off the table
and still couldn't get the tree to work.
It was only just now I thought of a way.

I dropped the wooden sheep from a few inches
above the table so they wouldn't bounce.
Some are on their backs but they serve
the same as the ones standing.
What I can't get over is their coming right
inadvertently when I'd be content with any solution.

Ah, world, I love you with all my heart.
Outside the open window, down near the Hudson,
I can hear a policeman talking to another
through the car radio. It's eleven stories down

so it must be pretty loud.
The sheep, the tree, the dog, and the man
are perfectly at peace. And my peace is at peace.
Time and the earth lie down wonderfully together.

The blacks probably do rape the whites in jail
as Bill said in the coffee shop watching the game
between Oakland and Cincinnati. And no doubt
Karl was right that we should have volunteered
as victims under the bombing of Hanoi.

A guy said to Mishkin, "If you've seen all that,
how can you go on saying you're happy?"

THE POET GOES ABOUT HER BUSINESS

for Michele (1966–1972)

Michele has become another dead little girl. An easy poem.
Instant Praxitelean. Instant seventy-five-year-old photograph
of my grandmother when she was a young woman with shadows
I imagine were blue around her eyes. The beauty of it.
Such guarded sweetness. What a greed of bruised gardenias.
Oh Christ, whose name rips silk, I have seen raw cypresses
so dark the mind comes to them without color.
Dark on the Greek hillside. Dark, volcanic, dry and stone.
Where the oldest women of the world are standing dressed in black
up in the branches of fig trees in the gorge
knocking with as much quickness as their weakness will allow.
Weakness which my heart must not confuse with tenderness.
And on the other side of the island a woman
walks up the path with a burden of leaves on her head,
guiding the goats with sounds she makes up,
and then makes up again. The other darkness is easy:
the men in the dreams who come in together to me with knives.
There are so many traps, and many look courageous.
The body goes into such raptures of obedience.
But the huge stones on the desert resemble
nobody's mother. I remember the snake.
After its skin had been cut away and it was dropped,
it started to move across the clearing.
Making its beautiful waving motion.
It was all meat and bone. Pretty soon it was covered with dust.
It seemed to know exactly where it wanted to go.
Toward any dark trees.

DIFFERENT NOT LESS

All of it changes at evening
equal to the darkening,
so that night-things may have their time.
Each gives over where its nature is essential.
The river loses all but a sound.
The bull keeps only its bulk.
Some things lose everything.
Colors are lost. And trees mostly.
At a time like this we do not doubt our dreams.
We believe the dead are standing along the other edge
of the river, but do not go to meet them.
Being no more powerful than they were before.
We see this change is for the good,
that there is completion, a coming around.
And we are glad for the amnesty.
Modestly we pass our dead in the dark,
and history—the Propylaea to the right
and above our heads. The sun, bull-black
and ready to return, holds back so the moon,
delicate and sweet, may finish her progress.
We look into the night, or death, our loss,
what is not given. We see another world alive
and our wholeness finishing.

TROUBLE IN THE PORTABLE MARRIAGE

"What whiteness will you add to this whiteness, what candor?"

We walk the dirt road toward town through the clear evening.
The sky is apricot behind the black cane. Pink above,
and dull raspberry on the Turkish hills across the water.
The Aegean is light by the shore, then dark farther out.
I cannot distinguish now which is light and which is color.
I go up the road on my bicycle, floating in the air:
the moon enlarging and decreasing, moving all the time
close to my head. I stop at the bridge.
Get off and sit on the rail because I remember
I have no money. After a while you come.
Your hand touches me and then withdraws.
We talk about why the moon changes size, and I think
how I'd smelled it. Like sweet leaf smoke,
like sweet wood burning. We go toward town together,
me riding and you walking. Feeling the silk and paleness
of the air. No one passes us the whole length of the road.

CLASSICISM

The nights are very clear in Greece.
When the moon is round we see it completely
and have no feeling.

WHOLE AND WITHOUT BLESSING

What is beautiful alters, has undertow.
Otherwise I have no tactics to begin with.
Femininity is a sickness. I open my eyes
out of this fever and see the meaning
of my life clearly. A thing like a hill.
I proclaim myself whole and without blessing,
or need to be blessed. A fish of my own
spirit. I belong to no one. I do not move.
Am not required to move. I lie naked on a sheet
and the indifferent sun warms me.
I was bred for slaughter, like the other
animals. To suffer exactly at the center,
where there are no clues except pleasure.

GROWING UP

I am reading Li Po. The TV is on
with the sound off.
I've seen this movie before.
I turn on the sound just for a moment
when the man says, "I love you."
Then turn it off and go on reading.

SUMMER IN A SMALL TOWN

When the men leave me,
they leave me in a beautiful place.
It is always late summer.
When I think of them now,
I think of the place.
And being happy alone afterwards.
This time it's Clinton, New York.
I swim in the public pool
at six when the other people
have gone home.
The sky is gray, the air hot.
I walk back across the mown lawn
loving the smell and the houses
so completely it leaves my heart empty.

No More Marriages

Well, there ain't going to be no more marriages.
And no goddam honeymoons. Not if I can help it.
Not that I don't like men,
being in bed with them and all. It's the rest.
And that's what happens, isn't it? All those people
that get littler together. I want things
to happen to me the proper size.
The moon and the salmon and me and the fir trees,
they're all the same size and they live together.
I'm the worse part, but mean no harm.
I might scare a deer, but I can walk and breathe
as quiet as a person can learn.
If I'm not like my grandmother's garden
that smelled sweet all over and was warm
as a river, I do go up the mountain
to see the birds close and look
at the moon just come visible, and lie down
to look at it with my face open.
Guilty or not, though, there won't be no post-
cards made up of my life with Delphi on them.
Not even if I have to eat alone all these years.
They're never going to do that to me.

EURYDICE

I linger, knowing you are eager (having seen
the strange world where I live)
to return to your friends
wearing the bells and singing the songs
which are my mourning.
With the water in them, with their strange rhythms.
I know you will not take me back.
Will take me almost to the world,
but not out to house, color, leaves.
Not to the sacred world that is so easy
for you, my love.

Inside my mind and my body is a darkness
which I am equal to, but my heart is not.
Yesterday you read the Troubadour poets
in the bathroom doorway
while I painted my eyes for the journey.
While I took tiredness away from my face,
you read of that singer in a garden
with the woman he swore to love forever.

You were always curious what love is like.
Wanted to meet me, not bring me home.
Now you whistle, putting together
the new words, learning the songs
to tell the others how far you traveled for me.
Singing of my desire to live.

Oh, if you knew what you do not know
I could be in the world remembering this.
I did not cry as much in the darkness
as I will when we part in the dimness
near the opening which is the way in for you
and was the way out for me, my love.

The Defeated

I sat at the desk for a while fooling with my hair
and looking at the black birds on the bakery roof.
Pulled the curtain, put my hair back, and said
it's time to start. Now it's after three.
You are still on the bus, I guess, looking out
the window. Sleeping. Knowing your defeat
and eating lunch part by part so it will last
the whole journey.

I heard there are women who light candles
and put them in the sand. Wade out in dresses
carrying flowers. Here we have no hope.
The pregnant woman has the abortion and then
refuses to speak. Horses stall in their strength,
whitening patches of air with their breath.
There will be this going on without them.
Dogs bark or five birds fly straight up
to a branch out of reach.

I had warm pumpernickel bread, cheese and chicken.
It is sunny outside. I miss you. My head is tired.
John was nice this morning. Already what I remember
most is the happiness of seeing you. Having tea.
Falling asleep. Waking up with you there awake
in the kitchen. It was like being alive twice.
I'll try to tell you better when I am stronger.

What does the moth think when the skin begins to split?
Is the air an astonishing pain? I keep seeing the arms

bent. The legs smashed up against the breasts,
with her sex showing. The weak hands clenched.
I see the sad, unused face. Then she starts to stand up
in the opening out. I know ground and trees.
I know air. But then everything else stops
because I don't know what happens after that.

Too Bright to See

Just before dark the light gets dark. Violet
where my hands pull weeds around the Solomon's seals.
I see with difficulty what before was easy.
Perceive what I saw before
but with more tight effort. I am moon
to what I am doing and what I was.
It is a real beauty that I lived
and dreamed would be, now know
but never then. Can tell by looking hard,
feeling which is weed and what is form.
My hands are intermediary. Neither lover
nor liar. Sweet being, if you are anywhere that hears,
come quickly. I weep, face set, no tears, mouth open.

The Apparent

When I say transparency, I don't mean seeing through.
I mean the way a symbol is made when an X is drawn over O.
As the world moves when it is named. In the sense
of truth by consciousness, which we translate as *opposites*.
The space we breathe is also called distance.
Presence gives. Absence allows and calls,
until Presence holds the invisible, weeping.
Transparent in the way the heart sees old leaves.
As we become more like the hills by feeling.
I mean permanence. As when the deer and I
regard each other. Ah, there was no fear then.
When she went with her young from the meadow
back into the nearly night of the woods,
it was because the rain came down suddenly harder.

THE GODS MUST NOT KNOW US

> The signifying clouds at dawn
> fill me. Open my spirit.
> The shining of sun and moon
> morning after morning
> makes my heart serene.
>
> (from *Shang-shu Ta Chuan* by Fu Sheng)

All the different kinds of light
give off light.
The light of the heart (sun).
The light of the mind (moon).
Longing and having make it all
possible for us.

But what the world gives disturbs,
this confusion of excess the world gives.
Morning comes again and again,
holding everything lovingly.
We cannot hold it all at once
this giving.

KALOS is written over the heads of the gods
on the Greek vases. They like beauty so much
they fill the world with it.
Until the plenty makes our joy hesitate
and I fear they will know we do not have a place
big enough to handle so much.

The world gives forth beauty
like the great, glad women in the dream.
It overwhelms us. Spills over.
I am afraid the earth will take it back
and part of myself will get lost
and I will not be a fitting gift.

The gods must not know us well or they would
not dance so openly, so happily before us.

THE GRUB

The almost transparent white grub moves
slowly along the edge of the frying pan.
The grease makes the only sound, loud
in the empty room. Even the rim is cooking him.
The worm stops. Raises his head slightly.
Lowers it, moving tentatively down the side.
He seems to be moving on his own time,
but he is falling by definition. He moves forward
touching the frying grease with his whole face.

This Place

There is a place in the desert which I keep making,
making the light blister and the shadows glow
with a red darkness. Making black a substance
invisible behind the red. Shadows
like those in a place built to be a stronghold
for pity's sake make me wonder why I put it there,
making sure of the heat and the blond lions
quivering against the blond sandstone so that
you almost cannot see them, or believe them
a mirage. Making water of them and moving them
closer to the rock. It makes me wonder why
I saw lions as guardians, angels flexing their jaws,
tightening against the walls for pity's sake.
And I cry out to them with my burned mouth
full of joy and wonder: "Pity, I have found you.
Pity, I bring you a present of my mind, complete
with the sweet smell of the King's garden
when you come into it from a small distance.
I have not made you up. You are here."
And the lions turn in the canyon I have made
with my voice, see me calling, and we move closer.

What If the World Stays Always Far Off

What if the world is taken from me?
If there is no recognition? My words unheard?
Keats wanted to write great poetry
and I am in the orchard all day.

The work is too hard and no one here
will do it. So they bring Jamaicans.
The men sometimes sing on their ladders.
Named Henry and George. "Yes, Boss," they say.
The bus brought them late this morning.
They not wanting to work because of the cold.
They walk slowly through the wet grass.
"Today we are not happy," they say going by me.

The grass is wet one to three hours.
Then dry. Sometimes everything is warm
and I wish the man I know would come
in his car and make love to me.

We do not speak much. Because of the work.
And because I am the only woman.
They see no women. Two months here picking apples.
Six in Florida cutting cane.

At night my body is so tired I don't want
to make love. I want to be alone and to sleep.
It is very beautiful in the fields under
the apple trees all day. I saw two night hawks,
white with black wave designs counter to the wings.

The boss saw two hundred of them fly over
this valley once. Going south.
What if I continue unnoticed.

Foxes red and gray. Woodchucks. A pretty rabbit
on the road in the rain, confused and afraid.
Running suddenly toward the lights.

An apple has all colors. Even blue.
Much purple and maroon. (If there would be
no recognition and the world remains far away?)
The leaves are a duller green than the grass.
I pick macintosh, but there are forty kinds
on the land around. Three hundred acres
near the next town. This is autumn in Massachusetts.
Not my home. I heard of beauty in New England
and the people. Came looking for love.

Nobody talks to the Jamaicans. They are driven
to Safeway in the bus and brought back.
I saw one alone just standing by the woods.
"I send money to my mother if I feel like it,"
he said to impress me. About eighteen.
He will cut cane for the first time this year.
"I hear the bosses are mean," I said.
"We make more money," he said. "It is a longer time."

Are you lost if there is no recognition?
Is beauty home? Is fear or pain?

An old man who drives the truck and has a farm
of his own down the road said,
"I just help during the harvest.
I have everything except apples. Lots of squash."
It made me happy to know they still say harvest.

I am here with them for the harvest. Thirty-six.
A woman. Canning when there's time. It will be
very cold soon. Already there are dark rains.

Sun Moon Kelp Flower or Goat

Later I would say, I have cut myself free from order,
statistics, and what not, what have you.
But I was never connected. To anything.
Marriage taught me to let go more. As if I knew
what I wanted. As if I were after something,
The *finally* was that year as I walked the island
every day. I could feel something extraordinary.
It was the same in me as outside me. I could say us:
the flat land I walked. The mountain approaching.
The blanching of everything living and dying.
Ruined hills and towns without roofs on the houses.
Men and women in black clothing offering water,
singing, being silent, laughing. Dying, as if that
were anything to us who were nature and beyond
suffering. What survives. The part which remains.
What is birth and death to sun, fish, kelp, eggs?
But there is kindness which feeds us another way,
with windlessness, empty heat, or the taste of grapes.

SKYLORD

for Harold Gregg (1906–1980)

The small hawk flutters fiercely upright,
shivering with great energy to stand so
in air over hills and their declivities.
Hunting mole, mouse and whom. Ally of wind,
owner of sky, elegant lord embracing what is
known and not known. A magnificence over us
which plunges for small life to eat. Dear gods,
you are dependent on the mouse that lives
with the hill's heartbeat and knows more,
much more by far, than your invisible school
of latitude and longitude. You must study
by compression of patience movement between
eyelids blinking. Must learn racing between
two heartbeats. And it takes you a long while
and humility and failure. Each time you come
close we look in awe of you. That the sky too
has its stomachs to feed and must come down
to us and learn our ways. For you do. With
splendor and work you learn how to kill and take
what you must while the salmon rot after spawning
in rain and in clarity. As we learn hovering
and density from your necessity. We learn
from you joy in the ground as you raise each
prey in your claws from the dear lost earth.

ALMA TO HER SISTER

alone no loneliness in the dream in the quiet
in the sunrise in the sunset Louise.
in the dream no loneliness in the dream
in the sunrise in the sunset just the two of us

alone no loneliness done. in the dream
in the quiet of the day done in the sunrise
Louise. in the dream in the dream
in the sunrise in the sunset.

alone no loneliness done. no loneliness
in the dream in the quiet
in the sunrise in the sunset. Louise
in the dream. in the sunrise in the sunset.

from *Alma*

At Home

Far is where I am near.
Far is where I live.
My house is in the far.
The night is still.
A dog barks from a farm.
A tiny dog not far below.
The bark is soft and small.
A lamp keeps the stars away.
If I go out there they are.

Safe and Beautiful

Moon, you are getting worse and worse.
Lying around in pretty satin,
your hair fixed all careful like a widow.
I capture this lizard and house it
in my hands. Feel the scratching.
We look at each other between my fingers,
he as Dante and I as the ghost,
the Lost-in-the-Night, the daughter
of faith built on common ground. While you,
old moon, play safe, safe, beautiful and safe.

The Ghosts Poem

I.

Heavy black birds flying away hard from trees
which are the color of rust that will green.
A smaller bird says his life is easy.
"I can fly over the water and return.
I feel very little. I see to it the dead
in the boats keep their arms crossed
in the correct position. They are shaken
by wind and the drift to leeward.
And when they arrive, I am there by the lilies.
I sing my highest song. They open their eyes
and memory is removed from them.
It is the final condition."

II.

I used to skate on the pond and now it is water.
With the sound of hammers and scythes, scythes
and hammers all around. So what do I know?
Laurie is dying. She told her husband she's tired
of fighting. He said he'll be glad when it's over.
They are giving her a mixture of heroin and morphine
so the mother says good-bye to her friends in euphoria.
What does she see? The Acropolis in moonlight before
it decreases? The kore which resembles most of what
we have to offer? Does death carry us to speak
with the invisible? Are we carried to an ocean
where water covers our feet and then withdraws,
leaving us shivering? What does history have to say?
"Empty rooms. The dead in layers."

III.

Ghosts and the old are gathered here.
Bored of being gathered without waltzes,
one asks for music and the bird says soon.
Spider comes and goes in her tunnel.
Lady, I ask, is it true you are cruel?
You are very busy. Do you make coverings
for us to wear? "I work for Death
and the power of men. If you want me less,
you know what to do," she answers.
But I am not persuaded. The sight of them
blind and groping fills me with pain.
I must help them down the stairs and on
their way. They are the best we had,
and among them are the bronze bells
of that deliberate passion which saves
what is perfection from ruin.

IV.

I go to the shore and say to Death,
here I am. What power do you have
if I care only for the living?
He shows me his skirt to be inviting.
He sings his loudest song. I sing low.
Death, I sing, you are not dear.
You are nothing but a hole in the ground.
"Watch your mouth," says the spider.
But I am too excited and tell him I have
music and memories. That men and women
embrace even in stone on the old tombs.

V.

Dirt road. Then under tall pines. Then grass.
Where the land slopes, the sun shines
and many flowers came up. Some right away,
some later, some finally.
While in that place which had been a pond.
There is a creek, and a dark hill of trees
beyond, with ferns from spring until October.
Last year I spent time there every day.
I weeded out the briars and my hands bled.
During the summer there were many snakes,
or one often. This is not a story.
This is how I lived. Morning glories covered
the wall, poppies lasted late into autumn.
This winter, when the snow thawed a little,
I saw through the ice the pansies.
They still had green leaves and stems
and the flowers were the same color as before.

VI.

The blackness at the window turned me back
to the fire. My heart praised its warmth
and the sound it made of a snake hissing,
as a man breathes out when struck. The room was
darkest in the corners where the ghosts were.
What is alive is everything, they said.
Death has you standing still, little sister.
We can help very little. Bird is the least
useful. Spider is really an old woman
who hides in the ground because she is poor.

But snake knows death. He has it both ways.
Escapes from his body and lives again.
His divisions and endings return on themselves.
See how he comes into the bright summer garden
when he has a choice. Snake is wonderful.

VII.

There must be more than just emotion.
Longing is enough to get me where I am,
but it cannot change me from a plant
that sings into a snake which sleeps
like a doe in the sun and then slides
into the blackness we balk from.
The resonance of romance brightens
the invisible so it can be seen.
We must ascend into light to be manifest.

VIII.

If we did not hold so much, I would not write.
If it were not for memories, for the ghosts
carrying the hundred clamoring moons,
I would be safe. The forests keep
saying I should not remember, but always
there is the sound of their breathing.
If it were all right just to love and die,
I would not be in this empty place
three stories up looking out on nothing
I know. If I could bind my mouth
or teach my heart despair of living,
I would not be here learning what to say.

Marriage and Midsummer's Night

It has been a long time now
since I stood in our dark room looking
across the court at my husband in her apartment.
Watched them make love.
She was perhaps more beautiful
from where I stood than to him.
I can say it now: she was like a vase
lit the way milky glass is lighted.
He looked more beautiful there
than I remember him the times
he entered my bed with the light behind.
It has been ten years since I sat
at the open window, my legs over the edge
and the knife close like a discarded idea.
Looked up at the Danish night,
that pale, pale sky where the birds that fly
at dawn flew on those days all night long,
black with the light behind. They were caught
by their instincts, unable to end their flight.

BALANCING EVERYTHING

When I lie in bed thinking of those years, I often
remember the ships. On the Aegean especially.
Especially at night among the islands or going
to Athens. The beauty of the moon and stillness.
How hard those journeys sometimes were.
The powerful smell of vomit and urine, sweetened
coffee and crude oil when the ship struggled
against the wind. I think of the night
we were going to die in the storm trying to reach
the passenger liner. Huge waves smashing
over our little boat. Jack screaming at the captain
because he hit me in his fear. Old Greek women
hiding their heads in my lap. Like a miracle.
I talked to them with the few words I knew.
Simple things. How it would be all right.
Telling them to look at the lights of their village
at the top of the great cliffs of Santorini,
up in the dark among the stars.

At the Gate in the Middle of My Life

I had come prepared to answer questions,
because it said there would be questions.
I could have danced or sung. Could have loved.
But it wanted intelligence. Now it asks
what can be understood but not explained
and I have nothing with me. I take off
my shoes and say this is a plate of food.
I say the wind is going the wrong way.
Say here is my face emerging into clear light
that misses the sea we departed from to join you.
Take off my jacket and say this is a goat alone.
It embraces me, weeping human tears. Dances
sadly three times around. Then three times more.

NOT SAYING MUCH

My father is dead and there is nothing left
now except ashes and a few photographs.
The men are together in the old pictures.
Two generations of them working and boxing
and playing fiddles. They were interested
mostly in how men were men. Muscle and size.
Played their music for women and the women
did not. The music of women was long ago.
Being together made the men believe somehow.
Something the United States of America could
not give them. Not even the Mississippi.
Not running away or the Civil War or farming
the plains. Not exploring or the dream of gold.
The music and standing that way together
seems to have worked. They married women
the way they made a living. And the women
married them back, without saying much,
not loving much, not singing ever.
Those I knew in California lived and died
in beauty and not enough money. But the beauty
was like a face with the teeth touching
under closed lips and the eyes still. The men
did not talk to them much, and neither time
nor that fine place gave them a sweetness.

OEDIPUS EXCEEDING

Finally Oedipus came back. Returned
as the old to the ancient. Found a stone
and sat down. Blind and blinding.
Slowly people gathered around him,
hesitant and horrified. He began.

The earth is winnowed, he said.
Put through a sieve. It is what happens
at the borders. A grinding away.
The ocean against the curving shore.
Sky against the mountain. Less rock.
Fewer trees. A reduction of whatever
bulges. A hammering.

Almost nothing of it is useful to us.
The ocean and sky laboring to make
their place. Salt wetness and the storm.
If we go forward, we go beyond.
If we return to the gentle green center,
we come back defeated. We are expected
to rejoice and grieve at the same moment.

A telling goes on at the border.
At the border an intermingling of fish
with swallow. Of eagle with hands.
I have returned to mix my blood with our
earth. Mix myself with what we are not.
(His voice in the crowd was like wind
blowing the chaff away.) There is a hole

in the ground behind this stone, he said,
through the bushes. I will go there now
and lie down forever.

The people walked back toward town.
Something had happened. Everything
was sacred. Air, goat, plants, people.
All full of worship. Bodies, torsos, legs,
minds full of worship. And strong enough
to be happy in the elements.

The Shopping-Bag Lady

You told people I would know easily what the murdered
lady had in her sack which could prove she was happy
more or less. As if they were a game, the old women
who carry all they own in bags, maybe proudly,
without homes we think except the streets.
But if I could guess (nothing in sets for example),
I would not. They are like those men who lay their
few things on the ground in a park at the end of Hester.
For sale perhaps, but who can tell? Like her way
of getting money. Never asking. Sideways and disconcerting.
With no thanks, only judgment. "You are a nice girl,"
one said as she moved away and then stopped in front
of a bum sitting on the bench who yelled that he would
kill her if she did not get away from him. She walked
at an angle not exactly away but until she was the same
distance from each of us. Stood still, looking down.
Standing in our attention as if it were a palpable thing.
Like the city itself or the cold winter. Holding her hands.
And if there was disgrace, it was God's. The failure
was ours as she remained quiet near the concrete wall
with cars coming and the sound of the subway filling
and fading in the most important place we have yet devised.

LIES AND LONGING

Half the women are asleep on the floor
on pieces of cardboard.
One is face down under a blanket
with her feet and ankle bracelet showing.
Her spear leans against the wall by her head
where she can reach it.
The woman who sits on a chair won't speak
because this is not her dress.
An old woman sings an Italian song in English
and says she wants her name in lights:
Faye Runaway. Tells about her grown children.
One asks for any kind of medicine.
One says she has a rock that means honor
and a piece of fur.
One woman's feet are wrapped in rags.
One keeps talking about how fat she is
so nobody will know she's pregnant.
They lie about getting letters.
One lies about a beautiful dead man.
One lies about Denver. Outside
it's Thirtieth Street and hot and no sun.

How the Joy of It Was Used Up Long Ago

No one standing.
No one for a long time.
The room is his room,
but he does not go there.
Because of the people.
He stands in the dark hall.
The smell makes him close
his eyes, but not move
from the place so near.
They have cut the cow open
and climb into the ooze
and pulse of its great body.
The man is noble, the festival
growing louder in his flesh.
His face is sad with thinking
of how to think about it,
while his mind is slipping
into the fat woman.
The one he saw for a moment
near day, open and asleep.
A filth on the floor of that room.

The Men Like Salmon

The heart does not want to go up.
The bones whip it there, driving it
with a terrible music of the spirit.
The flesh falls off like language,
bruised and sick. Sick with the bones.
Rotten with sorrow. Leaving everything
good or loved behind. The bones
want to go. To end like Christ.
Ah, the poor flesh. The mute sound
of flesh against stone. Emptied
of maidens and summer and all
the fine wantonness of life.
The bones insist on immaculate changes.
The women stand to the side remembering
Io with vicious flies close to her heart.

THE COPPERHEAD

Almost blind he takes the soft dying
into the muscle-hole of his haunting.
The huge jaws eyeing, the raised head sliding
back and forth, judging the exact place of his killing.
He does not know his burden. He is not so smart.
He does not know his feelings. He only knows
his sliding and the changing of his hunger.
He waits. He sleeps. He looks but does not know his
seeing. He only knows the smallness of a moving.
He does not see the fear of the trapping.
He only sees the moving. He does not feel the caution.
He does not question. He only feels the flexing
and rearing of his wanting. He goes forward
where he is eyeing and knows the fastness
of his mouthing. He does not see the quickness collapsing.
He does not see at all what he has done. He only feels
the newness of his insides. The soft thing moving.
He does not see the moving. He is busy coaxing
and dreaming and feeling the softness moving in him.
The inside of him feels like another world.
He takes the soft thing and coaxes it
away from his small knowing. He would turn in and follow,
hunt it deep within the dark hall of his fading knowing,
but he cannot. He knows that.
That he cannot go deep within his body for the finding
of the knowing. So he slows and lets go. And finds
with his eyes a moving. A small moving that he knows.

DEATH LOOKS DOWN

Death looks down on the salmon.
A male and female in two pools, one above
the other. The female turns back along the path
of water to the male, does not touch him,
and returns to the place she had been.

I know what death will do. Their bodies already
are sour and ragged. Blood has risen
to the surface under the scales. One side
of his jaw is unhinged. Death will pick them up.
Put them under his coat against his skin
and belt them there. Will walk away
up the path through the bay trees.
Through the dry grass of California to where
the mountain begins. Where a few deer
almost the color of the hills will look up
until he is under the trees again and the road ends
and there is a gate. He will climb over that
with his treasure. It
will be dark by then.

But for now he does nothing. He does not disturb
the silence at all. Nor the occasional sound
of leaves, of ferns touching, of grass or stream.
For now he looks down at the salmon large and whole
motionless days and nights in the cold water.
Lying still, always facing the constant motion.

NEW YORK ADDRESS

The sun had just gone out
and I was walking three miles to get home.
I wanted to die.
I couldn't think of words and I had no future
and I was coming down hard on everything.
My walk was terrible.
I didn't seem to have a heart at all
and my whole past seemed filled up.
So I started answering all the questions
regardless of consequence:
Yes I hate dark. No I love light. Yes I won't speak.
No I will write. Yes I will breed. No I won't love.
Yes I will bless. No I won't close. Yes I won't give.
Love is on the other side of the lake.
It is painful because the dark makes you hear
the water more. I accept all that.
And that we are not allowed romance but only its distance.
Having finished with it all, now I am not listening.
I wait for the silence to resume.

DRY GRASS & OLD COLOR OF THE FENCE
& SMOOTH HILLS

The women are at home in this California town.
The eucalyptus trees move against whiteness.
When a mother comes by I touch the child's face
over and over, sliding my hand lightly down,
and each time he smiles. All life is beautiful
at a distance. But when I sit in their houses,
it's all mess and canning and babies crying.
I hear over and over the stories about their men:
betrayal, indifference, power. Age without passion,
boys without fathers. My sister lives between.
She cleans her house. She names all the roses
she shows me. She turns on the record and we dance.
She inside with the door open, me on the porch.
Later her boyfriend arrives. The one who hits her,
and steals her money, and gets drunk. Etcetera.
They have sex. In the morning we're alone and she
wants to know if I want waffles with raspberry jam.

If Death Wants Me

If death wants me, let it come.
I am here in a room at night on my own.
The pulsing and the crickets would go on.
Everything and the tall trees bathed in darkness
would continue. I am here with the lights on
writing my last words. If he does not come,
I will still be here doing the same thing.
Things change outside of me. Rain is falling
fast in the quiet. My love got on a boat
and it went away. I stayed. When the moon rose,
I tilted my head to the side when she did.
When people came, I felt a little crazy.
I did what I remembered. Made food.
Asked questions and responded. And they left.
I would go to sleep and wake in the sun.
Love the day as if it were a host of memories,
then go to the wall and wait.
That hour was perhaps the finest of all.
No people. No bright face. No geese walking home.
No night sounds at all. I was silent
with all things around coming and leaving
in abeyance on their journeying. I would sing
a song for them all. This is for you
and this is for you. And then the moon would slide up
over the hill and I would be captured in her light
like a growing thing, gone and complete.

Praising Spring

The day is taken by each thing and grows complete.
I go out and come in and go out again,
confused by a beauty that knows nothing of delay,
rushing like fire. All things move faster
than time and make a stillness thereby. My mind
leans back and smiles, having nothing to say.
Even at night I go out with a light and look
at the growing. I kneel and look at one thing
at a time. A white spider on a peony bud.
I have nothing to give, and make a poor servant,
but I can praise the spring. Praise this wildness
that does not heed the hour. The doe that does not
stop at dark but continues to grow all night long.
The beauty in every degree of flourishing. Violets
lift to the rain and the brook gets louder than ever.
The old German farmer is asleep and the flowers go on
opening. There are stars. Mint grows high. Leaves
bend in the sunlight as the rain continues to fall.

from *The Sacraments of Desire*

GLISTENING

As I pull the bucket from the crude well,
the water changes from dark to a light
more silver than the sun. When I pour it
over my body that is standing in the dust
by the oleander bush, it sparkles easily
in the sunlight with an earnestness like
the spirit close up. The water magnifies
the sun all along the length of it.
Love is not less because of the spirit.
Delight does not make the heart childish.
We thought the blood thinned, our weight
lessened, that our substance was reduced
by simple happiness. The oleander is thick
with leaves and flowers because of spilled
water. Let the spirit marry the heart.
When I return naked to the stone porch,
there is no one to see me glistening.
But I look at the almond tree with its husks
cracking open in the heat. I look down
the whole mountain to the sea. Goats bleating
faintly and sometimes bells. I stand there
a long time with the sun and the quiet,
the earth moving slowly as I dry in the light.

ORDINARY SONGS

Dull with pneumonia, wrapped on the porch,
I watch the wind darken parts of the smooth sea
again and again. Watch the sheen return
each time a lighter color. The Greek woman
sings as if the sky were listening.
Ordinary songs. About a man gone long enough
for her to know he's gone always. Songs like that.
Sings easily and loud over the quiet water
to where the sky disappears. Sheep eating
and bells ringing. I think of the roofs
in Massachusetts with the gray sky above
and the blind man walking in the snow as the train
shook everything passing near us. I think of us
all wanting the gods to touch our skin. Our hearts
blessing the slender bare trees in American lots
of bearded dry weeds. I have come here
for the trial by grace, by loneliness. Remembering
the girl I started as trying to know the earth
with her body, the touch of the bark all she had.
Trying to find her way to the love women know.
I have brought myself to these hot fields of dark
red poppies and the quiet cove over there.
Shepherds and fishermen and the happy women
in black who give me milk and fish while everything
blooms and I accept gratefully. Listening to doves,
I grow sleepy and dream of a still world where space
looks like the sound owls make at night. A world
without color that knows the sea's dark blue.
Without people, but knows the dancer and marble form.

Without light, but knows the fire it came from.
I sleep as a shard weary from earthquakes moving earth
an inch at a time, tilting each thing. The sea
wearing away the land. Everything stronger than me.
On the shard a reclining naked woman kissed by a god.

SURROUNDED BY SHEEP AND LOW GROUND

When death comes, we take off our clothes
and gather everything we left behind:
what is dark, broken, touched with shame.
When Death demands we give an accounting,
naked we present our lives in bundles.
See how much these weigh, we tell him,
refusing to deny what we have lived.
Everything that is touched by light
loves the light. We the stubborn-as-grass,
we who reel at the taste of sap and want
our spirits cleansed, will not betray
the weeds, snake, or crippled mare.
Never leave behind what the light shone on.

The Small Thing Love Is

My body is filled by a summer of lust
and I can't tell the difference between desire,
longing, and all the sweet speeches
love hoards. Something deeper grinds its teeth
on metal, mocks and preens in cold rooms
where a glass breaks and women wear
rich gowns that weigh more than they do.
Death mating with Beauty. Night roaring
and the cathedral holding its ground
against the strength and purring
of the wet couple undone
by a power only the earth could love.

Ahdaam Kai Ava

I came the whole way around from going out
to cliffs and oceans and edges
where I stood with all my strength
begging and singing and weeping, and came back
to this makeshift farmyard where my little ones
sleep in the toilet at night with the door
held closed with a rock. They dance
with webbed feet all day in the water.
They begin to sing as soon as I let them
out into the morning; and no matter what
I am or how I feel, my heart no bigger
than theirs refuses to keep still and I
listen intently. Harmonize in the silence
of myself with their unimportance:
their elegant, unimportant happiness.

All the Spring Lends Itself to Her

If Her skirt does not bend the grass, nor sea air
mold Her shape while She is happy, there is no grace.
I will not stop looking for that. Song and color
circle in this air for Her to stand in.
If She does not come to take pleasure in this giving,
all things will reverse to alms and penitence.
She is not needed for this world to be a success.
Either way the other powers will have their time.
But if spring comes and She is absent, we will eat
food without sacrament, our hearts not renewed
for the other seasons: the one where we give, the one
where we are taken, and the season where we are lost
in the darkness. If love does not reign,
we are unsuited for the season of ripeness.
If we do not see Her body in the glass of this beauty,
the sun will blind us. We will lie in the humming fields
and call to Her, coaxing Her back. We will lie
pressed close to the earth, calling Her name,
wondering if it is Her voice we are whispering.

NIGHT MUSIC

She sits on the mountain that is her home
and the landscapes slide away. One goes down
and then up to the monastery. One drops away
to a winnowing ring and a farmhouse where a girl
and her mother are hanging the laundry.
There's a tiny port in the distance where
the shore reaches the water. She is numb
and clear because of the grieving in that world.
She thinks of the bandits and soldiers who
return to the places they have destroyed.
Who plant trees and build walls and play music
in the village square evening after evening,
believing the mothers of the boys they killed
and the women they raped will eventually come
out of the white houses in their black dresses
to sit with their children and the old.
Will listen to the music with unreadable eyes.

The Design inside Them

At six every night the women sit on chairs
under vine leaves or out on the street in front
of the houses on whitewashed rocks crocheting.
The talk in Greek is too fast for me, but I can tell
it is about prices in Mytilene compared to here.
They make pictures of flowers and leaves and birds
with white string to cover the windows,
tables and pillows. One of the women serves me
a piece of cake in syrup and a glass of water.
A daughter comes through the billowing curtain
in the doorway. She is fifteen and wants a Walkman
and goes away. She will never be like them.
Her little sister goes from the mother and stands
near a man who is feeding olive branches to his goat.
Then to the new kittens and back to her mother.
Sits quiet in the chatter and industry, and then away
again to the kittens and the man. As though
a string is tied to her waist and unravels like
their idea of justice and good and gentle kindness.
Gathers up again as the old swallows and flowers.

In Dirt under Olive Trees
on the Hill at Evening

Her naked body is too small for the woman's head.
The face tilts away as it listens to the music
She makes, the expression perfect happiness.
A diadem and curly hair with bits of gold
and white and red paint. The only wing left
curves from Her shoulder like the tail of a horse
prancing. Why do we care so much about the grace
of winged women, singing naked or lightly clothed?
Made by men to what purpose? A rock would do
as well, or some broken weeds. Why not the smell
of earth warmed all day by the sun, or the sense
of unseen water underground, or the sky at morning?
Why this pity, this glad humming when we see Her
sitting with tinted breasts on a little clay throne?

NOT SCATTERED VARIOUSLY FAR

I keep saying, "Is She here? Is that Her?"
Whatever I see. Knowing I am not far off
that way. Not far wrong. But I want more.
To see Her again. On a little clay throne
with fruit or bird. Some white on Her breasts,
pink on Her skirt. A vastness around.
I will tell Her I am here already dead.
I will bring Her my story of loss
like a broken toy and see it mended
miraculously in Her hands.
She will be smiling all the time,
gentle and glad. I will tell Her
Mother hurts me, has always saddened me.
She will tell of trouble with Her mother.
While birds sing. It will be enough.

A Dark Thing inside the Day

So many want to be lifted by song and dancing,
and this morning it is easy to understand.
I write in the sound of chirping birds hidden
in the almond trees, the almonds still green
and thriving in the foliage. Up the street,
a man is hammering to make a new house as doves
continue their cooing forever. Bees humming
and high above that a brilliant clear sky.
The roses are blooming and I smell the sweetness.
Everything desirable is here already in abundance.
And the sea. The dark thing is hardly visible
in the leaves, under the sheen. We sleep easily.
So I bring no sad stories to warn the heart.
All the flowers are adult this year. The good
world gives and the white doves praise all of it.

The Last Night in Mithymna

Wind heaving in the trees.
My room quiet and warm.
Me on a thin mattress
looking at the full moon.
The sky black around Her face.
The trees a different black
beneath. Content at last
with this world that matches
my life inside and out.
Heave and renewed heave
inside and out,
and the gentleness.
Lying alone in a cotton slip
at ten of the night in July
and a bare bulb hanging down
turned on. My bare feet
warm where they cross
at the ankle.
The cloth over the broken window
swells and goes flat
and swells again.

PART OF ME WANTING EVERYTHING TO LIVE

This New England kind of love reminds me
of the potted chrysanthemum my husband
gave me. I cared for it faithfully,
turning the pot a quarter turn each day
as it sat by the window. Until the blossoms
hung with broken necks on the dry stems.
Cut off the dead parts and watched
green leaves begin, new buds open.
Thinking the chrysanthemum would not die
unless I forced it to. The new flowers
were smaller and smaller, resembling
little eyes awake and alone in the dark.
I was offended by the lessening,
by the cheap renewal. By a going on
that gradually left the important behind.
But now it's different. I want the large
and near, and endings more final. If it must
be winter, let it be absolutely winter.

The Color of Many Deer Running

The air fresh, as it has been for days.
Upper sky lavender. Deer on the far hill.
The farm woman said they would be gone
when I got there as I started down the lane.
Jumped the stream. Went under great eucalyptus
where the ground was stamped bare by two bulls
who watched from the other side of their field.
The young deer were playing as the old ate
or guarded. Then all were gone, leaping.
Except one looking down from the top.
The ending made me glad. I turned toward
the red sky and ran back down to the farm,
the man, the woman, and the young calves.
Thinking that as I grow older I will lose
my color. Will turn tan and gray like the deer.
Not one deer, but when many of them run away.

Grinding the Lens

I am pulling myself together.
Don't want to go on a trip.
I have painted the living room white
and taken out most of my things.
The room has never been so empty.
Just now a banging thunder
and suddenly falling rain.
I leave the typewriter and run
outside in my nightgown and take
the cotton blanket off the line.
It is summer and I am in the middle
of my life. Alone and happy.

SINGING ENOUGH TO FEEL THE RAIN

I am alone writing as quickly as I can,
dulled by being awake at four in the morning.
Between the past and future, without a life,
writing on the line I walk between death
and youth, between having and loss.
Passion and bravery absolutes, and I don't
have anything but the memory of Aphrodite's
elbow pushing up through the dirt, golden
with the sunlight on it. I am far from there
in a hurry not to miss the joining,
struggling to explain that this worse time
is important. It is just past autumn now
and the leaves are down, wet on the road.
Some of Her shoulder showed, but not enough
to tell whether She was facing my way.
Any of it is most of it, as any part
of Cézanne is almost all of Cézanne. Now
is so late in the world that there is silence.
Heart is as beautiful as ever. What can we
expect of a woman buried in the earth?
Most of it is enough. Some of it is almost
enough. Just as I am a body too, and if he
leans down over me there will be a world.
A train goes past making an incidental sound.
Something is nourished by the loss. An ending
and beginning at once. The world does not sing,
but we do. I sing to lessen the suffering,
thinking of the factory girl Hopkins said
lived a long time on the sacrament alone.
But I also sing to inhabit this abundance.

THE WAR

We were at the border and they were checking
the luggage. We had been talking about Lermontov's
novel, *A Hero of Our Time.* John liked Petorin
because he was so modern during that transition
from one history to another. I talked about Vera
and Princess Mary, the old man and the others
Petorin hurt. I said there was no reckoning for him,
that he was not held accountable as in Tolstoy
or Dostoevsky. Maybe morality does change,
I was thinking, but suffering does not. Then
a scorpion crawled from a bundle on the table.
He fell to the floor and scurried across the room.
The men were delighted. One crouched down and held
the scorpion with a ballpoint pen while he cut off
the poisoned stinger at the end of the tail,
the scorpion stretched out was as long as a hand.
The men gathered around, some with open pocketknives
held shoulder high. The man picked up the scorpion
by the tail and put it on his friend who yelped,
jumping away. The men laughed. The scorpion fell.
Another man picked it up and threw it lightly
against the wall. The scorpion fell and kept trying,
scuttling across the tiles toward the open door.
He kept his tail high, threatening, but looked tired.
Somebody else picked up the scorpion and I told John
I was going. We went outside where there was nothing.

The Foreign Language of the Heart

Rivas said the virgin sisters went singing across
the empty countryside, each of them dressed in white,
full of desire for the lover who had not yet come.
I see women everywhere seeking a love that changes
but never grows less. If they went away, they have
returned. Returned unchanged, but dressed in black.
If you are carrying something on your head in a bag,
one will seek you out later when you are resting.
If you are indifferent, a young woman startles you
awake early in the morning and you hear different
kinds of birds singing in the four trees. If you
still do not respond, there will be an old woman
in the hot streets wearing a dirty gray dress.
If there is nothing that can stir you, you will see
a thin, very tall Indian woman sitting every day
with her bags on the wide steps of Iglesia El Carmen
just outside the big doors accepting alms,
watching with no particular expression as you pass.

THE LIFE OF LITERATURE

Very early in the morning at the edge of the capital
she is trying to get a ride. The huge machines
go past noisily, covering her with dust. She worries
about finding safe water or soda on the way.
Finally a man reaches down and helps her climb up
the wheel and over the side into the bed of the truck.
A young girl shifts to make room, then settles her
small brother's head in her lap. An old man turns
the blade of his machete away from them. When she
reaches Condega it is a quiet town. That night
she sits on a piece of cardboard in the garden
behind the house with the husband who used to live
with her. They look at the moon and talk
of poems in the book she lent him. The one
by Bashō called *The Long Road into the Deep North.*

Inside the War

The muzak is loud, full of sighs and bongos
in the neon light, with me in a corner by the window.
I order papaya juice because it comes in bottles. A kid
is selling plastic bags of unshelled peanuts which are
threaded to a wire ring he wears on his shoulder.
A boy wants to shine shoes. A man sells little sacks
of cookies and of saltines. I buy crackers. Outside
it is getting dark. The owner tells the kid to leave.
One sells Chicklets, another cigarettes. Some people
go out and a boy pours himself water from the pitcher
on their table. The others are still, watching him drink,
then all the boys go to the far end of the restaurant.
A woman comes in and sells lottery tickets. Three men
come in with an accordion and two guitars. They walk
around in the din of muzak carrying their instruments.
I feel sorry for them, but the muzak stops and they sing
La Paloma while the boy shines shoes at a table of men
and beers and hot sauce, the white tablecloth with plastic
over it. Koo-koo-roo-koo, they sing, then sing it again.
Ya-ya-ya-yoo. Four musicians come in with three guitars
and a gourd shaker. They chat with people and watch
the trio who are singing louder and louder. I am eating
heavy chop suey made mostly of cabbage. The boy selling
Chicklets comes over, but I say no. He looks at my food
and I ask if he wants to eat. He picks up my plate,
puts it on the other side of the table and sits down.
He quickly eats the cabbage and the bread and drinks
the rest of the papaya juice. All the musicians are singing

the Mexican music, taking turns. The lights go out and oil
lamps are brought in. I walk back to my apartment through
the dying city, using my flashlight because it is
the turn of my district to have the electricity turned off.

There Is No Language in This Country

Poetry is not in Puerto Sandino. The men stop working
at noon and silently, together, with space around
each one, walk to the Comedor to eat without forks,
spoons or knives (because they were stolen once).
A few men have tablespoons in their back pocket,
the others eat with their fingers. A place where
the water must come from somewhere else to make
the fruit drinks. Or in Tamarindo where the children
who have desks carry them home on their heads
because the school has no windows or doors. They
come running to you with the cries of children who
think nothing of living in fire. All wanting their picture
taken together under the ruined tree. There is shyness
in the ones who come close, but none of this is real.
Reality is the dust color and the boy sitting alone
at the center of a bench alongside the house, one
foot on the bench in front of him, his arm wrapped
around that leg, hand cupped over his mouth,
looking at me and the scene. That is more like it.
Or the man in a hammock lying absolutely still with
his eyes open. There is a place where you can buy
beer along the road where it turns off to enter
La Paz Centro, but only those with money go there.
Cigarettes and things that people want are nowhere
else. In town, the huge doors of the church are open.
The floor is clean, but there are no people. Poetry
does not live here, unless poetry truly is
on the side of things that have no language.

Like the earth, or people who live below the line
of existence. Poetry is the voice of what has no voice
to tell the difference between sand and dirt, rocks
and heat, life and death, love and this other thing.

The Border between Things

Our meetings are like hawks mating, you said,
plunging straight for the earth, crying for
extra distance. Falling faster, the ground
very near. Simplifying in the wild rush of air.
When I was a child at Playland, we cranked
the old movies by hand. When we paused, a man
stopped. If we turned more, the man walked out
into the ordinary night of a small town
and a few cars. (I imagined cricket sounds.)
The stuttering of the scene, the constant
jerking made it somehow more real, made it
more seeable. Everything for us now is blurred
by our passion. Your shoes drop on the floor
and we immediately are together, blessed
and unreal in the rapid going forward. And yet
we search for evidence of the partial thing.
Afterwards, I stand at the window tilting
a black and white negative in the light, trying
to make it positive. Wondering if God prefers
the flickering as we cross the border from dark
to invisible. From not having to being undone.
Do we pass from loneliness to beyond without
hovering between? Leda remembered nothing
but the ecstasy. Not the gradations of tenderness
and muscle. She remembered just before, remembered
spreading her knees and the ecstasy raining down.
But not the border, not the zig-zagging back
and forth between the visible and the invisible.
Not the moment between the natural and unnatural.

It Is the Rising I Love

As long as I struggle to float above the ground
and fail, there is reason for this poetry.
On the stone back of Ludovici's throne, Venus
is rising from the water. Her face and arms
are raised, and the two women trained in the ways
of the world help her rise, covering her
nakedness with a cloth at the same time.
It is the rising I love, from no matter what element
to the one above. She from water to land,
me from earth to air as if I had a soul.
Helped by prayers and not by women, I say
(ascending in all my sexual glamour), see my body
bathed in light and air. See me rise like a flame,
like the sun, moon, stars, birds, wind. In light.
In dark. But I never achieve it. I get on my knees
this gray April to see if open crocuses have a smell.
I must live in the suffering and desire of what
rises and falls. The terrible blind grinding
of gears against our bodies and lives.

THE SONG

The bird is not smart. The heart
rules her as the sun does,
as the tree she lives in rules her.
Who is to say it should be different?
She does not question. She sits
on the sway of branch at evening
and knows how to distinguish
one calling from all the other
songs at the end of each day,
in the very last light.

Demon-Catchers on Our Doors

We walk up the valley ankle-deep in tenderness,
hunting lions without weapons. Knowing
what ripens desires to be gathered.
Ladies winnow at the threshing ring
on late summer days of singing and thirst.
It is what our strength tells us.
We gather sticks for the ritual,
the sound of animals in the air.
It takes strength to yield, to give in
to the applause of ocean and fire,
to let the bones dictate. They have been
in exile getting strength from the wildness.
We throw flowers on whatever that thing is
that roars, our hearts in our bodies.
It is right. The stars reel in the dark.
Vermeer's woman holds up the scale
to weigh the pearls in the quiet room.
And each time something happens
to make them balance in the satin light.

from *Chosen by the Lion*

The Ninth Dawn

It is not for nothing we notice a wider theme
in Virgil's *Georgics* when he speaks about
the passion of Orpheus and Eurydice. The gods
want the honey in the hive, are willing to have
the lovers destroyed. There is a grand design
pulsing around their perishing. A great sound
in which we can barely hear the lovers crying
each other's name. It doesn't matter that Procne's
bloodstained hands left marks on her breasts.
Virgil writes of important troubles: a country
at war, droughts and plagues, suffering and wrongs.
But the gods are interested in the honey, their minds
filled with the smell of burning thyme used
to fumigate the hives. I am haunted by Eurydice
who merely went too far into the woods and after
lived with the darkness around her forever.
I think of her loss and crying out as I listen
day and night to the man upstairs whose cries
of pain are like a wounded animal unable to do
anything but suffer. The gods instruct us to cut
the throats of eight beasts, throw in poppies,
kill the jet-black ewe in the beautiful Italian
light so the bees, who have been the real business
all along, will swarm out again under the pliant boughs.

God's Places

Does the soul care about the mightiness
of this love? No. The soul is a place
and love must find its way there.
A fisherman on his boat swung a string
of fish around his head and threw it
across the water where it landed at my feet.
That was a place. One day I walked into
a village that was all ruins. It was noon.
Nobody was there, the roofs were gone,
the silence was heavy. A man came out,
gradually other people, but no one spoke.
Then somebody gave me a glass of water
with a lump of jam on a spoon in it.
It was a place, one of God's places,
but love was not with me. I breathed
the way grape vines live and give in
to the whole dream of being and not being.
The soul must be experienced to be achieved.
If you love me as much as you say you
love me, stay. Let us make a place
of that ripeness the soul speaks about.

THE WEIGHT

Two horses were put together in the same paddock.
Night and day. In the night and in the day
wet from heat and the chill of the wind
on it. Muzzle to water, snorting, head swinging
and the taste of bay in the shadowed air.
The dignity of being. They slept that way,
knowing each other always.
Withers quivering for a moment,
fetlock and the proud rise at the base of the tail,
width of back. The volume of them, and each other's weight.
Fences were nothing compared to that.
People were nothing. They slept standing,
their throats curved against the other's rump.
They breathed against each other,
whinnied and stomped.
There are things they did that I do not know.
The privacy of them had a river in it.
Had our universe in it. And the way
its border looks back at us with its light.
This was finally their freedom.
The freedom an oak tree knows.
That is built at night by stars.

The Spirit and What Is Left Behind
(after Giotto)

One holding the feet, one the hands, another with her
back turned who faces his sex. One holding the head
and one more. Five women, all with the same grief.
Now with the new body of Christ. The body without
God inside. The spirit exited, Jesus all body now.

God's life with Christ was like the long capturing
of a fish. The fish now lying on a table and the room
radiant, voices saying hallelujah over and over,
the voices overlapping, like birds flying, a screen
of them to see through. There are times when the body
tries to exist on earth by itself. There are common
places left for this. But the spirit must enter
the body. The body must yield to it as much as cows
and palm branches do, each filled with the spirit
in order to become fully its own form. How gently
I remember each one of them.

                              As I remember the lover.
Without the spirit, the apartment changed back
to a ruined place, cheap, in an old building there
in an undesirable district of the city. And empty
now except for what I left behind: chair, table,
double bed, chest, window screen. I remember counting
the windows across the street to remember. Eight
were bricked-up, and three left as windows. I wanted
to keep even that. The body wanted to exist with
the spirit inside of it. Desire and hope spoke

constantly around us, the air always busy with that
celebration. Nothing was wrong. It was not wrong then.
But then there was death. Instead of life there were
only a few days at a time. Soon there were only hours.

Five women, three with haloes, around the dead Christ.
All expressing exactly the same grief. And Christ,
having yielded his spirit back to God, sinking back
into flesh while the Creator felt the spirit leaving
the body cell by cell, feeling the loss. Jesus was
whole for a while, and now will know only matter.
(But will know a difference: women and men, bodies
touching bodies.) The ones left behind will worry
about the flesh, the matter, will bury him. Will say
he rose again. Those on Earth use feelings to emulate
and understand. For now they wail, holding the clay-
colored body, lifting it with their hands, pulling it
by the wrists, his heels resting in palms, the body
slumped. By itself the body could not achieve enough.

I would be lying on the bed when I heard his key
in the lock. I would not stand up, would listen
to every sound: door opening, door shut. Perhaps
his voice saying my name, perhaps not. Then seeing
his face, at last for the first and only time, briefly,
briefly.

CHOSEN BY THE LION

I am the one chosen by the lion at sundown
and dragged back from the shining water.
Yanked back to bushes and torn open, blood
blazing at the throat and breast of me.
Taken as meat. Devoured as spirit by spirit.
The others will return quickly to drink again
peacefully, but for me now there is only faith.
Only the fact that the tall windows I lived
with were left uncovered halfway up.
And the silence of those days I lived there
which were marked by your arrivals like
stations on a long journey. You write to say
you love me and lie awake in stillness
to avoid the pain. I remember looking
at you from within at the last moment,
with faith like a gift handkerchief, delicate
and almost fragile. This is the final thing.
Purity and faith, power and blood. Is there
nothing to see? Not memory even of forgetting?
Only the body eating the body? What of faith
when it meets death, being when it is hard
to account for? The nipples you bit
and the body you possessed lie buried in you.
My faith shines as the moon in the darkness
on water, as the sky in the day. Does it hover
in the air around you? Does it come like
a flower in your groin? Or is it like before
when you were alone and about to fall asleep
saying out loud in the darkness, "Linda,"
and hearing me answer immediately, "Yes!"

OFFICIAL LOVE STORY

There is a painting by Lucas Cranach
of a thing pink and white and motionless.
Nymph of the Spring. A young woman
stretched out naked against
her red robes which are bundled
behind her head and arm, casually,
to resemble an open rose.
A pair of plump quail in the foreground
echoing her breasts and belly.
A sacred pool with water spilling down
into it from a small cave darkened
like her mystery. She considers
with her young, elegant mind
the sound of the water on water.
Always smiling,
her eyes looking down.
Probably there is the sound of horns.
Everything in the best
German tradition.
The cream of her being.
The world slow with desire.
Passion announced by the shadows
everywhere in the picture.
Soon a perfect prince will come
with shining arms and black hair,
and oriental eyes. He will beg her
for the flower of her body.
She will consider it with her neat mind
which smells of lemon,

the way roses smell. Everybody will clap,
wanting the world to be made
out of passion and grace.
The voices of children will sing sweetly
of Christ in his loss and fear,
sing of the birth after,
sing of the Mystery to come.

The Terrifying Power of Darkness
Is Inseparable from the Redemptive
Power of the Sacred

"Listen (Kirillov said) to a great idea: there was
a day on earth," etcetera. "Today thou shalt
be with me in Paradise," etcetera. "Both died
and . . . found neither Paradise nor . . . . Listen:
that Man was the loftiest of all on earth,"
and so on. "If the laws of nature did not spare
even Him, not spare even their miracle . . .
and made even Him live in a lie and die for a lie . . ."
and so forth. August nineteenth. A hurricane
is headed straight for Rhode Island at twenty
miles an hour with winds of a hundred and fifteen
miles an hour inside while Susan is there
with her three children. Hard rain here all day,
big breathing noises and strong freshness, hollow
and cleansing. This is a thousand miles from
where you are celebrating your birthday, moving
away from love and suffering. It is over, killed.
Siren sounds in this small city. In Russia,
this morning a coup. The question of whether
the military will fire on the people. It is not
reading of Proust's two uneven stones on the floor
of St. Mark's in Venice that makes me remember you
and struggle with the question of Faith.
It is the terrible balance I experienced with you
between love and evil. Jack says, "It was true,
but he couldn't sustain the love when it started
to cost him." Altizer says, speaking of Dostoevsky:

"The terrifying power of darkness is inseparable from
the redemptive power of the sacred, the deeper we are
drawn into the creative depths of darkness the more
real the actual presence of the sacred becomes."
It is the pain that makes me remember you. It is
the duration of this suffering that makes me look
back through the brutal phone call, an empty room,
my body silent as the silence I am in: your voice
not your voice, your words not your words. Back
to you dismantling a grapefruit piece by piece,
taking off the membrane of each and putting the fruit
in my mouth. I always thought joy was the way
we were supposed to feel, was the ordinary,
and that everything else was strange.
I believe that being requires the other, and the sacred
requires the thing. But I am alone. I must discover
my heart against rock. If you do this to me, if you
do this to me, if you take your love away, if you take,
if you go away, you will make my heart blind in me.

I Thought on His Desire for Three Days

"I draw circles around me and holy boundries"

Nietzsche

I chose this man, consciously, deliberately.
I thought on his desire for three days
and then said yes. In return, it was summer.
We lay on the grass in the dark and he placed
his hand on my stomach while the others
sang quietly. It was prodigious to know
his eagerness. It made me smile calmly.
That was the merging of opposite powers.
He followed me everywhere, from room to room.
Every single thing was joyous: storms, meals,
the story about the face that was the world.
There was the sound of Chicago buses stopping
near my house according to winter, summer,
raining. Shadows moved over the floor
as the sun went across the sky. I was a secret
there because you were married. I am here
to tell you I did not mind. Existence
was more valuable than that. When I was
a very young woman, I wrote: *A new spirit /*
I have a new spirit / I made it myself / I dance
now alone before the mirror / There is a flower /
The leaves are a little sad / No light comes
out of the black part / with its five purple
dots of color / near the center / Oh, my dead thing /
I have a new spirit / I made it myself. In Chicago,
a police siren ran through my heart even though

it was not for me. I was strong. I knew where
I was. I knew what I had achieved. When the wife
called and said I was a whore, I was quiet,
but inside I said, "perhaps." It has been raining
all night. Summer rain. The liveliness of it keeps
me awake. I am so happy to have lived.

The Clapping

Did I go there enough? Was it enough when I tried
to get there? I remember the view of the bay,
but not what was said when I got there.
Was waiting in that apartment all summer and all
winter an end in itself? Was it the secrecy
that mattered? I remember the life. You carrying
a bowl of soup you made (with oysters in it)
carefully across two rooms to give me, not spilling
any. There is the memory of me by the door. A memory
about summer darkness under a tree, and one of birds
in a bush as soon as it got light. I remember
sitting on the stairs after I gave up our place,
pressing my eyes against your stomach with your
open coat covering each side of my face. Pictures
mixed with blank pages like quiet mixed with silence,
light mixed with snow, sun on glass. And the heart
never tired, the passion never lessened. Eyes open
and mouth closed, mouth open and eyes closed.
I imagine my bicycle leaning on the outside steps
that lead to your door. You recognize it as mine
and move it while thinking about that boatload
of people all clapping as you embrace me on shore.
Which shore? Was there an earth? There was,
there was. There were streets. There was you
over me on the bed with all your clothes on,
even your winter coat and scarf. You naked another
time, sitting cross-legged on the bed happily clapping
at me. Loving everything, even the kitchen table.
Saying *now,* and *now,* and later *forever.* You and I
innocent in purity and magnificent disorder.

ASKING FOR DIRECTIONS

We could have been mistaken for a married couple
riding on the train from Manhattan to Chicago
that last time we were together. I remember
looking out the window and praising the beauty
of the ordinary: the in-between places, the world
with its back turned to us, the small neglected
stations of our history. I slept across your
chest and stomach without asking permission
because they were the last hours. There was
a smell to the sheepskin lining of your new
Chinese vest that I didn't recognize. I felt
it deliberately. I woke early and asked you
to come with me for coffee. You said, sleep more,
and I said we only had one hour and you came.
We didn't say much after that. In the station,
you took your things and handed me the vest,
then left as we had planned. So you would have
ten minutes to meet your family and leave.
I stood by the seat dazed by exhaustion
and the absoluteness of the end, so still I was
aware of myself breathing. I put on the vest
and my coat, got my bag and, turning, saw you
through the dirty window standing outside looking
up at me. We looked at each other without any
expression at all. Invisible, unnoticed, still.
That moment is what I will tell of as proof
that you loved me permanently. After that I was
a woman alone carrying her bag, asking a worker
which direction to walk to find a taxi.

THE RESURRECTION

Let the tower in your city burn. Let the steps
to the shadowed building by the lake burn
even though it is made of stone. Let the lion
house burn so that the roaring and burning
will be heard together. Let the old, poor
wooden house where I lived go up in flames, even though
you returned and sat on the steps that led
up to where we used to exist. Let it all burn,
not to destroy them, but to give them the life
my life gives to them now. To make them flare
as they do in me, bright and hot, bright and burning.

Aphrodite and the Nature of Art

I want a net made of iron to hold
what I am. I love artifice.
Hephaestus made the net that hoisted up
his wife, Aphrodite, and her lover.
Caught them in their gleaming hardness,
all ecstasy and soft, most secret flesh.
Good, she thought, at the root of her being
as she locked her ankles around the gardenia
that she is. While the two men yelled
at each other, the women filed out of the room
full of chaos as well as shape. Their husbands
stood amazed at what they were seeing,
the wonderful fish-like economy of her lower back,
seeing the links pressed into her body's delight
and leaving the imprint rose-colored on her
pale flesh. Hair swelling through some of the gaps
as the crippled maker raised them like a masterpiece
higher in the half-light of the vast room.

Winter Light

The way you fell asleep inside my breathing
and I watched your forehead, cheek and lips!
(What if I had loved myself more?)
The rush of you entering my heart's form!
Afterwards, tearing up pictures and things
was like fire. I loved you too much.
(I made a whole room fine with the single lily,
the whole room fine with emptiness and one flower.)
You cried, love me, love me, love me, love me!
Here, I said, take this and this, yes, all.
(Would you still be here if I had loved myself
a little? The stillness, the quiet,
even the tenderness, still here?)
You said you were confused, really confused.
(I did have a chair, did have that picture
of Picasso, Lady with a Fan. In profile,
one hand up, the other down. The one in front
of her showing its palm. So like the Amida Nyorai
who takes the souls into paradise. If I had
made a world, would you have lived there?)
The women in the beautiful paintings never have
broken hearts. They are happy in spring light,
standing in their gardens.
(If I had made a garden. If I had stayed happy.)

THE LOST BELLS OF HEAVEN

Helpless, the one and then the other,
so dear to each they folded round
each other for comfort and care.
Folded and foundered, they burrowed deep
into one another and made a room
in the air benevolent toward its lovers.
Interior it was, with bells constantly
ringing of blessing, blessing those
who dwell in the heart that is God's love.
So easy to tell, the blessing and bells,
the odor and moisture given out
like light into the air. Blessing
the curtain that half covered the darkness
of the blackened lightwell, and the window
open a crack and the door always only
almost closed. Dear God, how you loved
us then. What joy rose from our bodies
clenched together as it rained in that part
of Chicago with the bells ringing one
and then another when they rang. What a happiness
you are, Lover of thunder, Lord of the cripples,
Lord of the helpless, naked, starved and lost.

There Is a Sweetness in It

The sap rises in the maple each spring after
the squeeze and release, squeeze and release
of winter. The spirit rises up into the face
of a shepherd, light shining on his clothes
and legs, on his sheep, on the ground and on
the stranger standing nearby. Bodies, light,
sap, our language. The body and the spirit.
Would God put himself into the body of a man
if what he wanted was to escape from the body?
What if God wanted the tree to blossom simply
because it would be covered with purple flowers
without leaves as I remember seeing in Nicaragua?
The raised arms of a shepherd, the light
lighter at the horizon of black hills. Moonlight
falling passionately on the stranger passing
the roadside gravestone. God trying to get down
to squeeze him in the dark. God cannot stop.
God is there and always sees the black ball
the crescent moon is holding. Sees the old tree
bent over by the storm in a field of wheat
lit up like the ocean. His grip is suffering,
revelation is the release. The sap rises up
in man and beasts, and in all things vegetable.
Plants and animals do it even better, kneeling
or celebrating or shining more immediately
than men do. But God loves us more, because
of the dread and seeking we contain. He loves
our lostness because it is by loneliness
and sacrifice, our body and soul together, that

the thing God is can exist. We are the stone
that is sacred. The way we make love with each
other is the collision that makes His face shine.
Makes the sap rise. God squeezes and relents
like winter ending, and the sap rising.

FISHING IN THE KEEP OF SILENCE

There is a hush now while the hills rise up
and God is going to sleep. He trusts the ship
of Heaven to take over and proceed beautifully
as he lies dreaming in the lap of the world.
He knows the owls will guard the sweetness
of the soul in their massive keep of silence,
looking out with eyes open or closed over
the length of Tomales Bay that the egrets
conform to, whitely broad in flight, white
and slim in standing. God, who thinks about
poetry all the time, breathes happily as He
repeats to Himself: there are fish in the net,
lots of fish this time in the net of the heart.

"Wherefore Dost Bruise Me?"
He Exclaimed, Weeping, and
Like a Corpse Fell to the Ground

In the museum print room today we looked
at their Blake engravings. All were
about a place that was not Paradise.
Everybody suffering. Men on their backs,
their faces upside-down and exposed,
legs raised and merging with the lines
that meant a mountain.
Women, unusually large, stood composed,
discerning, concerned over the general
condition of life. The curator said,
"He cut directly into the metal."
"Then inked it," I said. "Yes," she said.
There was a spiral of mist
filled with the shapes of lovers.
I looked close to see if any were happy.
At least two were. And in the sky,
a couple sitting, embracing.
(Something weeps in me all the time.
All the time.) I said, at random,
"Wouldn't it be nice if one of these
prints showed an angel crossing the border
between heaven and this other realm.
Just the border."
(Jesus, you who are above all others,
I hurt constantly inside.
Bleared with loneliness.
Exhausted by keeping what I love safe.)

"A Bracelet of Bright Hair about the Bone"

The Romans put skulls into their love poems.
Skeletons and dry bones along with love.
As if violet was only beautiful against
something black. We also talked of death,
I perhaps more than you. It made me happy
to think of the newly dead body being lowered
into the coffin of the other. You found
this idea impressive but terrible.
I longed for your agreement and approval.
Wanted you to understand the hugeness of love.
You whispered that our bones would be mixed
together, but probably it was your way
to get me to stop crying and go to sleep.
Which I did, contentedly. I wanted something
to be done, some enactment to prove this secret,
this illicit love. Something too large.
I wanted it made of actual things. Dirt
and corpses even. As real as the table you
said your love was, that I could sit down to
and eat from if I wanted something permanent.
I wanted absoluteness to be made of my heart.

Maybe Leave-Taking

The birds eat the pansies as soon as they open,
and I almost smile. Perhaps I never cared enough
about these earthly things, about desire.
The sliding of seasons, coming and going,
youth and age. Sailing away sounds good to me.
Going away, always leaving. If I cried,
perhaps it was in relief and joy.
The lights on ships, light in the sky,
the lights of Patmos receding. All the people
strangers, people I do not know. A truer sense
of being than lovers and friends.
It is good to let go. Like all of me
pouring into a poem or dance. Leave-takings,
strangers, transfigurations. Not perishing,
but sailing away as I did that year
from Lesbos toward the coast of Turkey
and seeing a small boat near the shore
with a lateen sail, as if all the centuries could
arise and fall back. Only the flight of the single
spirit saved. Only the spirit having a heart
after all, and not what eats and is eaten away.

THE EDGE OF SOMETHING

I have decided I will not be like John Hu anymore
taken to France in the seventeenth century
and strange to everyone. Dragging his mattress
off the bed, sleeping by the open window in winter,
standing in the garden looking at the full moon
with his arms stretched out. Now I have chosen
Po Chü-i with his three pine trees and idleness
trying for union with the everlasting things.
As Po, I will not tell of the terrible things you did,
though I do not forget and still suffer.
When Po Chü-i was unhappy, he could still write,
"Narcissus are blooming in my backyard." The tulips
are not open yet, but the green is turning red.
I will not go out to see them in the morning.
I sleep late to allow my dreams luxury
and go out when the sun is starting down.
Afterwards, I practice my Chinese characters,
taking pleasure in feeling my mind yield
to what the symbols mean. This is *her,*
this is *him.* This one I think means *car.*
Later, I eat tofu and rice with cold asparagus
in a sauce of sesame oil, soy and white vinegar
with a little sugar. No more seabirds screeching
"Kiss the feet, kiss the fingers and the teeth.
Kiss the skull washed up on the beach. Kiss it,
kiss it, or you will be taken by dwarfs to the woods
where your love perches calling your name in the dark."
There is a great director in New York recovering
from a stroke who says, "Tea yes? Tea no? Music

yes? Music no?" Substance without outline.
When the deer on this summer mountain raise
their ears and look my way, I stop—knowing they will run
if I don't. A family of animals all of a kind.
We are the same in the same world. Same color
and stillness. Similar in our foreignness.
Foreignness married by air. This is as close
as we will come. This is the edge of not running.

THE BOUNTY AFTER THE BOUNTY

It is all in not having.
A mountain of three goddesses
without goddesses. Where they had been.
Gone, but truer therefore.
The absence, the loss creates a truth.
They go away, but something remains.
They remain. It is their absence
that I find, that I hold onto.
Having is the mistaken focus of desire.
It is not the point. The statue is
camouflage for the emptiness left behind.
It is a location for the intensity.
Where snakes had been under the stone.
People, dolphins, trees
all disturb the world with their presence.
The heart was wrong. It only wanted milk.
The soul was wrong with its gossip
and energy. The geometry of Islam
is the language of the hidden.
Our failure is our love for the world.
Our failure was thinking Christ
was His presence.
We were blinded by the actual body
of Jesus. He struggles,
it struggles to hold out against our will.

LET BIRDS

Eight deer on the slope
in the summer morning mist.
The night sky blue.
Me like a mare let out to pasture.
The Tao does not console me.
I was given the Way
in the milk of childhood.
Breathing it waking and sleeping.
But now there is no amazing smell
of sperm on my thighs,
no spreading it on my stomach
to show pleasure.
I will never give up longing.
I will let my hair stay long.
The rain proclaims these trees,
the trees tell of the sun.
Let birds, let birds.
Let leaf be passion.
Let jaw, let teeth, let tongue be
between us. Let joy.
Let entering. Let rage and calm join.
Let quail come.
Let winter impress you. Let spring.
Allow the lost ocean to wake in you.
Let the mare in the field
in the summer morning mist
make you whinny. Make you come
to the fence and whinny. Let birds.

from *Things and Flesh*

The Precision

There is a modesty in nature. In the small
of it and in the strongest. The leaf moves
just the amount the breeze indicates
and nothing more. In the power of lust, too,
there can be a quiet and clarity, a fusion
of exact moments. There is a silence of it
inside the thundering. And when the body swoons,
it is because the heart knows its truth.
There is directness and equipoise in the fervor,
just as the greatest turmoil has precision.
Like the discretion a tornado has when it tears
down building after building, house by house.
It is enough, Kafka said, that the arrow fit
exactly into the wound that it makes. I think
about my body in love as I look down on these
lavish apple trees and the workers moving
with skill from one to the next, singing.

ALONE WITH THE GODDESS

The young men ride their horses fast
on the wet sand of Parangtritis.
Back and forth, with the water sliding
up to them and away.
This is the sea where the goddess lives,
angry, her lover taken away.
Don't wear red, don't wear green here,
the people say. Do not swim in the sea.
Give her an offering.
I give a coconut to protect
the man I love. The water pushes it back.
I wade out and throw it farther.
"The goddess does not accept your gift,"
an old woman says.
I say perhaps she likes me
and we are playing a game.
The old woman is silent,
the horses wear blinders of cloth,
the young men exalt in their bodies,
not seeing right or left, pretending
to be brave. Sliding on and off
their beautiful horses
on the wet beach at Parangtritis.

THE CALVES NOT CHOSEN

The mind goes *caw, caw, caw, caw,*
dark and fast. The orphan heart
cries out, "Save me. Purchase me
as the sun makes the fruit ripe.
I am one with them and cannot feed
on winter dawns." The black birds
are wrangling in the fields
and have no kindness, all sinew
and stick bones. Both male and female.
Their eyes are careless of cold and rain,
of both day and night. They love nothing
and are murderous with each other.
All things of the world are bowing
or being taken away. Only a few calves
will be chosen, the rest sold for meat.
The sound of the wind grows bigger
than the tree it's in, lessens only
to increase. *Haw, haw,* the crows call,
awake or asleep, in white, in black.

CALAMITIES: ANOTHER EDEN

Out beyond what we imagine.
Out beyond the familiar, leaving home
and being homeless. Breaching the seas,
foundering on a coast in the West,
searching along coastlines in the Far East.
The heart is left and leaves,
stands in each part of the farness
away from the other. Living in each
particular moment of the day,
of present claims and the careless claims
of always. The ocean pushes out,
pushes the heart into the unknown,
toward the middle of a self that yearns
and remembers. The spirit is rejected
and walks slowly out of another Eden.
An Eden that is not the heart,
is homelessness, is isolate. The heart
is gathered into the familiar nothingness
and held. Is held and sent forth.
In the way a seal drops into the water,
sliding like oil in its element.
Turns and rolls. What we call happiness.
The seasons change and change,
west and east, tropical and far
northern. What we call love.
Heaven is deep and deeper. We leave
and leave into the questing.

THE SPIRIT NEITHER SORTS NOR SEPARATES

There is a flower. We call it God.
It closes and opens and dies.
We still call it God. There is a stone
that does nothing and is still God.
Everything is of Heaven. There is mud
around the edge of the pond.
There are reeds, water lilies
and a few dragonflies. The pond is light
and dark and warm because of the sun.
Hidden fish. The air itself.
The bush outside is full of three and four
kinds of birds. Winter birds instead
of leaves. The snow over ground is enough.
The birds hopping and feeding
and departing are flowers,
a mouth singing, your heart the way it was.

As Being Is Eternal

She is sitting alone in the bright room.
There are two other rooms, one dark
and closed, the other with a single light.
Outside there is a cold November.
She is remembering the statues
she saw in Greece on the mountain,
in empty rooms where light was added
to light, surrounded by silence.
They seemed ready to be seen.
The way one hears a door quietly
close and footsteps coming closer.
Present and past like that. The way
art is exact. Like the woman
in her lighted room.
She could rise and walk
into one of the empty rooms
that she is not in. Could see
a vase of red roses on the table
where white roses were last week.
Time has finished its journey,
has come its long half way.
The air is heavy as water as she
bends her head over the page.

The Heart Flowing Out

All things we see are the shapes death makes.
When we see straightly and hard we see
with the eyes of death. Light and dark, the weight
of the forms: a bell, a door, in their placement
one with the other. The black window
and the white wall are taut in their exact
distance, and firm in themselves,
surrounded by the imperfect dark hills
and the absolute light of the sky. Feeling is not
in the things, but in us. Though sometimes
they shake like a vision in their perfect tension
of being. Death is strong, so the world is
that strong too. A man walks down a road
then cuts across a field. We walk
with our soft bodies and tough minds.
Water is the shine moving, death does not flow.
We flow, our bodies and hearts flow.
When we enter death it gives way,
but not yet. Our hearts flow out through
the consciousness, focused.
The more it looks, the more it sees the hard
thing shaking with its own energy
in relation to the whole scene and its meaning.
Making that meaning, whatever it means.

The Empty Bowl

You know when to wake me in the dark
of the soul, your people singing a drone
without doctrine: *a lamb, a lamb, a lamb,*
a lamb. You know when to open our hands
and let what we are holding fall down.
Show us as you did in the ripe fields after.
The children crying in the garden,
lamb, lamb. Without residue, without humility.
Your voice, voices. Your voices'
voice. You know when to make the rain,
when to ask for our preparing. We stand
in line with the others, moving forward
without song, without understanding the words.
Love like a bowl, a trial to teach us
how to survive the sweeping, the breaking,
holding in the hands what is cherished
even in its uselessness, even as the bowl
of the mind disappears in the distance,
in the unvisited house where there is
no honey, no bees, the comb dead.
There is only the beginning of each day
with the roosters calling and our voice.
No salt, no bread. Only the chanting:
lamb, lamb, lamb.

MORE THAN NEW

One of the men begins to sing. The woman
turns from side to side, flouncing her skirt
and stomping. The men play their guitars.
He begins to sing again. She stamps harder
but it is not big enough. The man sings
so hard it breaks the song and becomes wailing.
The woman is proud. The men are proud.
Everybody is proud. And it is still not
strong enough. The gods are relaxed, pleased,
but justice is unmoved. Says, "Show me something.
Don't mess with me. Show me something I can believe."

ETIOLOGY

Cruelty made me. Cruelty and the sweet smelling earth,
and the wet scent of bay. The heave in the rumps
of horses galloping. Heaven forbid that my body not
perish with the rest. I have smelled the rotten wood
after rain and watched maggots writhe on
dead animals. I have lifted the dead owl while it
was still warm. Heaven forbid that I should be saved.

Another Day in Paradise

It is seven o'clock this morning.
Jeni looks up and smiles. Ti is scrubbing clothes
on her knees out back. Bu Fat is hardly visible
in the unlit kitchen. Lili picks up the tray
by the open doorway. Jeni is grinding a sauce.
Ti is dumping water from a plastic bucket
with one hand, making a splashing sound on cement.
Bu Su walks as if balancing something on her head.
Jeni smiles and speaks very slowly without sound.
Lili is cutting pork fat into small squares
on the bench. Ti is on her knees washing dishes.
Bu Fat is folding wontons close up to the counter.
Bu Su is carrying a tray of dirty dishes
into the kitchen without any expression.
Jeni stirs the pork frying in the wok. Lili is
cutting vegetables. Bu Su is frying onions
and laying them out to drain. The rice is steaming.
Ti is carrying a tray of food. Bu Fat is lifting
water from the reservoir in the kitchen. Someone
is sweeping. Two are washing the floor on their knees
with their backs to me, side by side. All have taken
baths with cold water and are wearing nice clothes.
All of them waiting in the big, now-empty restaurant.
They sit together at one of the tables. *Tedour,*
I say. Jeni says *Tedour* without making any sound.
One says, *Salammat Malan* and I say the same.
It is nine o'clock. They walk out into the dark night.

Heavy with Things and Flesh

Crowing. And a neighbor man already up.
Sun in the air above water.
Sunlight on a rock wall.
Sunlight on my floor.
Wind in the heat. A woman
in her farmhouse talking
to someone outside. Along with
hobbled goats in a field.
At eight in the evening
a man in his heavy wooden boat
is repairing the holes in
the yellow net piled around him.
I came here exhausted in my heart.
And will go back the same way.
The gods do sit at our table.
But when they leave, we don't follow.

A Thirst Against

There is a hunger for order,
but a thirst against. What if
every time a flower forms in the mind,
something gives it away to time?
Leaf by petal, by leaf. As if the soul
were a blotter of this world—
of the greater, the wetter, the more
tired, the more torn. All singing,
but no song. Hamlet darker than night.
And poor Ophelia less than the flowers
she wore. Both lost. One dead,
the other to follow soon.
One too heavy, one too frail.
Both finding themselves among the fallen.
Each time I think, it is here
that God lives. Right around here,
in this terrible, ruined place
with streets made desolate by neon,
in midwinter and freezing winds.
In these Chicago avenues.

THE LIMITS OF DESIRE

Love came along and said, "I know,
I know. Abandoned after all
those promises.
But I can't help. I traffic
in desire, passion, and lust.
Trade bread for more bread,
change blood into wine.
I take the heaviest things
and make them joyous."
We sit under the fig tree.
How fragrant she is, her hand
over the folds of her dress.
Head bowed, voice quiet
in the warm wind.

ALWAYS MISTAKEN

We see the ocean and hear
its noise as two different things.
We know they should be experienced
at the same time, but no one understands
how to do it. We can't decide whether
to be instructed by the white birds
flying ("Going to the source,"
as someone says), or to see them
as another aimless beauty
to be remembered with pleasure.
Everybody has a subject and they
take turns: peaches, new clothes,
lying naked alone on the porch
with the sun. Horses in shade
under bay trees by the creek.
Sex and kissing at the same time.
We never understood the life
we lived, nor the one now.
There is a clue. On Earth, the dance.
In Heaven, a table set with bowls
of rice and cups of tea.

THEY TELL ME IT'S OVER

I say, "I stayed in Motel 6, where you told me
to stay." He says, "I meant The Chicago Inn."
That was this winter's visit. That was a year.

Arkansas Afternoons

Today I took the postmaster's advice and found
Nina May, "who will talk to anyone," he said.
I needed to find how to get my quilt-tops backed.
Following his map, I drove behind Goshen
to the small square and the dots
that meant pine trees. There she was
in her house that looked out on fields.
She draped the four tops over a card table
and named each design: bow tie, snail,
nines. Then told me the story of how
she almost died a week ago.
She showed me a big pot of turnips she was
cooking, gave me the recipe. Gave me a glass
of Dr Pepper. Answered the phone
and told a sick friend she would call back
if her mind held out. She never answered
any of my questions about the quilts.
Said she would take care of them after
she got well, that we could go to see her
friend Pearl, did I want her to mend
the old tops. Went on about the blue
and yellow. "One might look good with
an edge that had a small design to balance
the top's boldness," she said.
I was saying inside, "Good-bye, good-bye,
my love. The great love of my life."
Waving like an Italian woman,
shamelessly. Knowing everything was lost
four years ago. Waving to no one now.

"WHY DOES THIS CITY STILL RETAIN / ITS ANCIENT RIGHTS OVER MY THOUGHTS AND FEELINGS?"

Osip Mandelstam

I did not tell you because I thought
it was a story, and I don't tell stories.
And because it isn't quite a story.
Misha was there on the couch
next to Joseph. When he crossed
the living room, I touched the soft leather
of his shoe. But that's not the story.
I did not think of it until now.
They sat together, two expatriates
talking in Russian about how to design
his *Nutcracker*. Misha would get up
and dance a passage or two, then sit down
and talk some more. They already knew
life was tragic. That was their weight.
Yet it was different with them.
They knew and were still capable. Even now
when Joseph is dead and Misha's not
dancing much. But what I wanted
to tell you about was not that.
What I wanted to tell you was after
that when they were talking Russian again.

STUFF

High up there she saw what
survives in the violent sunlight.
And felt no particular emotion.
The sea below, stone.

Circle that.

The wind in the bright heat
made a sound like winter.
The wind moving strongly
in the whitening wild wheat.

Circle *whitening.*

Goat, poppies, dry creek bed.

Circle all of it.

Parts of sentences: *bleached*
in the thin far-away,
momentary, and.
A veil in her mind moved,
momentarily uncovering
memory and *of.* She felt
dazed by *facts* and *cared-for.*

Circle *facts.*

THE UNKNOWING

I lie in the palm of its hand. I wake in the quiet,
separate from the air that's moving the trees outside.
I walk on its path, fall asleep in its darkness.
Loud sounds produce this silence. One of the markers
of the unknown, a thing in itself. To say
When I was in love gives birth to something else.
I walk on its path. The food I put in my mouth.
The girl I was riding her horse is not a memory
of desire. It is the place where the unknown
was hovering. The shadow in the cleavage
where two mountains met. The dark trees
and the shade and moving shadows there
where the top of the mountain stops and meets
the light much bigger than it is.
Its weight against all the light. A birthplace
of the unknown, the quick, the invisible.
I would get off my horse and lie down there,
let the wind from the ocean blow the high grass over
my body, be hidden with it, be one of its secrets.

FIEFDOM

In the tea garden of the Muslim graveyard
(three small tables with chairs) the clamor
of Istanbul is dulled by the trees
and simplicity, and the stillness
of the dead people below. An old man comes
to take the order for the only thing he sells.
Returns with two glasses of bitter tea,
two cubes of sugar and a small tin spoon
on each saucer. The quiet is in the idea
of silence. Like the heavy iron fence
all around, and the cat who runs away
into her world of stone paths, tombs,
dirt, bushes, and her small sounds.

THE UNIVERSE ON ITS OWN

Nature without shape, the universe without form.
Rubble, mistakes, lies, things thrown away.
Shapes we can only guess at. Leveled, broken,
strewn, lost. Maybe the picture on a shard
of a young goat hanging from somebody's shoulder.
Maybe only a black triangle with white splotches
overlapping like swarms in the sky at night,
like bees looking for a new home. The shape of love
is a scattering. The meaning we resist. The world
as far as we can see random in a wind.

DOWNSIZED

She lives where no one comes to visit.
In an old house made of stone and wood,
with bamboo ceilings. When she goes down
to the village, she says good evening
in a foreign language to the old people
sitting outside on the streets of rock.
They are the only words she speaks all day.
This morning when she opened
his letter to read again, a scorpion
fell out on her white cotton nightgown.
"Each day," she thinks later, "I am less
and less part of the world, even though
I live closer to it than ever."

Paul on the Road to Damascus

The soul is an emblem so bright
you close your eyes. As when the sun
here comes up out of the sea and blazes
on the white of a village called Lefkes.
The soul is dark in its nature, but shines.
A rooster crows. The tall grass
stirs on the ruined ancient terraces.
The shadow of a wafting crocheted curtain
runs in a slant down the wall of a house
as the Albanians paving the street below
are banging pieces of marble
against a metal wheelbarrow.

Hephaestus Alone

His heart is like a boat that sets forth alone
on the ocean and goes far out from him
as Aphrodite proceeds on her pleasure journeys.
He pours the gold down the runnels
into a great mystery under the sand.
When he pulls it up by the feet
and knocks off the scale, it is a god.
What is it she finds with those men
that equals this dark birthing? He makes
each immortal manifest. The deities
remain invisible in their pretty gardens
of grass and violets, of daffodils and jasmine.
Even his wife lives like that. Going on yachts,
speaking to the captains in the familiar.
Let them have it, the noons and rain and joy.
He makes a world here out of frog songs
and packed earth. He made his wife
so she contains the green-fleshed
melons of Lindos, thalo blue of the sea,
and one ripe peach at five in the morning.
He fashioned her by the rules, with love,
made her with rage and disillusion.

THE RIGHT PEOPLE

I liked everything about the gods.
Strong naked men in the clearest light,
women with their breasts showing.
And the way their thin gowns
draped, the layering and flow.
Interested in passion rather than exceeding.
Willing to understand nothing about love.
Which is why I am looking
at the flowering caper bush
that contains what I know about the Earth
creating the eternal out of itself
without rising above or letting go.

The Secrets of Poetry

Very long ago when the exquisite celadon bowl
that was the mikado's favorite cup got broken,
no one in Japan had the skill and courage
to mend it. So the pieces were taken back
to China with a plea to the emperor
that it be repaired. When the bowl returned,
it was held together with heavy iron staples.
The letter with it said they could not make it
more perfect. Which turned out to be true.

Harmonica

Gone like the fish in water
The rock on the road
A dove on the sill of the soul

Love is gone like a rock in water
A dove in the air
Sun that was on the mountain

Fish up the stream
Buckeyes flowering
Horse on the hill

House on the other side
of the hill

LOST IN THE HEART

The crazy woman at the beginning of the mountain
spends her days on the dirt road,
her face painted white. A man walks by
with his arms raised, holding empty
cigarette packages, the back of his pants ripped
and his underpants torn, showing the brown skin
of his bottom. Safety is not the answer.
Nor loving kindness. So I leave
Kuan Yin's temple to protect the loneliness
of each one there. The soiled moon is one
day too old. What was easy to pity
is no longer fine. The world is stronger
than ideas about the world. I walk home
knowing the moon rides the night as strongly
as ever. But my heart does not look up.

WINNING

There is having by having
and having by remembering.
All of it a glory, but what is past
is the treasure. What remains.
What is worn is what has lived.
Death is too familiar, even though
it adds weight. Passion adds size
but allows too much harm.
There is a poetry that asks for
this life of silence in midday.
A branch of geranium in a glass
that might root. Poems of time
now and time then, each
containing the other carefully.

^{from} *In the Middle Distance*

The Lightning

The bell ringing has been a great pleasure
for her during these months. But she
has been confused by the many secrets.
The fragments of stories between
upstairs and down. Like when the woman
dressed in such a beautiful white gown
with only one shoe. And that one with
no heel. And the other woman upstairs
and down. Fragments of stories.
She admitted it was her fault because
of her questions. Dreaming her own story
wanting to be part of it. And never explained.
The strange life she would take upstairs
and the waiting. The lightning in the night
over Iowa cornfields. Talking about love
and its dangers. About what happens when
you lay the new image over the old.

Purity

I'm walking on farm road 2810 again,
alone as always. Unless you want to count
the Border Patrol. Or the police cars
that go by with their strange maneuvers
in front of me and pull off into
the mowed grass on the side. Then turn
and come back. Stalling and facing me.
Waiting until a car approaches
from far away. It passes and the police
follow it toward town. Leaving me
with animals, insects and birds.
And the silence. I walk toward the sun
which is always going down.

Staying After

I grew up with horses and poems
when that was the time for that.
Then Ginsberg and Orlovsky
in the Fillmore West when
everybody was dancing. I sat
in the balcony with my legs
pushed through the railing,
watching Janis Joplin sing.
Women have houses now, and children.
I live alone in a kind of luxury.
I wake when I feel like it,
read what Rilke wrote to Tsvetaeva.
At night I watch the apartments
whose windows are still lit
after midnight. I fell in love.
I believed people. And even now
I love the yellow light shining
down on the dirty brick wall.

Elegance

All that is uncared for.
Left alone in the stillness
in that pure silence married
to the stillness of nature.
A door off its hinges,
shade and shadows in an empty room.
Leaks for light. Raw where
the tin roof rusted through.
The rustle of weeds in their
different kinds of air in the mornings,
year after year.
A pecan tree, and the house
made out of mud bricks. Accurate
and unexpected beauty, rattling
and singing. If not to the sun,
then to nothing and to no one.

GETTING VALUE

My elderly friend of many years arrived
last winter at my door with his nose
dripping onto the floor, and shaking
so hard you could hear his teeth clatter.
It was hard to get his clothes off
and him onto the sofa bed in my living room.
Filling me with memories of what
he used to be. What the French call
"monsters." (Like Rodin.) His poetry is
deeper now. Bigger, and more tender
than ever. We wonder about the newness
of the old. And how much is missing.
He forgets names and directions.
Surely there is a hollowing out,
but how much that is left is more than
the past was? The Shakespeare who stopped
writing. And the crippled Leonardo.
What about our very old god who is
now making his problematical children?

As Is

Pay attention, talk to no one unless
you are buying food or borrowing a book.
Or asking for directions to the border,
or the canyon, or the river with a pool.
Always formal. Poor with poor.
It's not the same here. No Greek ruins.
No fragment with legs of walking horses
painted delicately on it. No part
of a lion on bits of a glazed vase.
Like a code to tell of the world they knew
would be destroyed. Here there is no need.
The rabbit's groin is ripped open
on the road. When you find a bird's wing
there is a flattened small bird attached.
A ranch at evening, the sun leaving,
antelope standing and the other birds
flying. All of it meaning the same thing.

THE OTHER EXCITEMENT

If I go back into memory it's not
because I like it, but because
that's where the hard things are.
Nothing that gets excited. Almost
ripe and the beauty of things
in the middle distance.
Going down the mountain.

THE OTHERNESS

Of course there is the otherness,
right away inside you when
the doe steps carefully down
the embankment. Then clatter
of hoof and the dappled water
with leaf shade. The otherness
and the invisible until you came.

THE PROBLEM OF SENTENCES

A sentence is an idea. An idea with urgency.
A feeling for the sun before it rises.
The imagination loves the wall of a building,
loves the floor and the square window
that looks out on it. The scent of jasmine
is how the plant climbs up the wall
built by the Knights of Rhodes.
But the sentence stresses the meaning,
making us notice an unruly jasmine against
the orderly stone wall. We say our bus
went down through the village of the insane,
or that the eucalyptus trees were tall.
That we saw a man dragging a big branch.
The sun will return whether you smile or cry,
clap or burn candles. But when I say *whether,*
the sentence may be thinking, *even so.*

BEAUTY

There she was on *Entertainment Tonight*.
Someone had caught a glimpse of Bardot
after all these years. Brigitte Bardot
running through the trees, across a meadow,
a dog running with her. The hair still long.
Then another part showing her on the patio,
aged. (Sun-damaged, we say.) The violation
of beauty never happens just once.
When my father heard his beloved dog
had chased and killed the rancher's sheep,
he went right out and shot it. Because,
he said, once they ran with the pack
and tasted blood, it would never stop.

WAITING

When I chewed a bay leaf and rubbed
sage on my hands and arms, I believed
it was in order not to scare the deer.
Which was true. Later I thought it was
so my soul could be read by God.
Now I suspect it was a way for me
to become hidden. When you came to court me
for my body and hair, I was not there,
even though I was washed and dressed
for the occasion. Did you see me stare
beneath the courtesies? I was waiting
for someone to want that. To want
the moon by itself. For the quiet
of the herd. Of the stones under the water
in the creek flickering. Seeming to move,
but not moving. Together with everything
that's here.

The Presence in Absence

Poetry is not made of words.
I can say it's January when
it's August. I can say, "The scent
of wisteria on the second floor
of my grandmother's house
with the door open onto the porch
in Petaluma," while I'm living
an hour's drive from the Mexican
border town of Ojinaga.
It is possible to be with someone
who is gone. Like the silence which
continues here in the desert while
the night train passes through Marfa
louder and louder, like the dogs whining
and barking after the train is gone.

After the Fires

Now that you are old, you have moved inland,
surrounded by trees and a river hidden below.
You walk there with your life inside you.
The scenes, the arrangements and dissertations
on the bounty of women, the flecks of their color,
and all the rest. With your age upon you,
your boxes of papers and pictures cut out of
the *National Geographic* ranging from the forties
to the present, to know the world that was yours.
It makes me remember the fires that were built
on the beaches when I was young. Huge fires
made out of what was there. I remember what
they looked like when the fires went out.
Plenty of logs left blackened, held by the wet
and high tides. I stand with the size
of the burnt-out fires the morning after
and listen to the quiet young ocean.

Silence and Glare

I get out of the car. Stand still
and listen. Look at the abandoned house,
generally. Has the plaster fallen off?
If so, how long have the adobe bricks
been exposed to rain? A house
made of mud and straw otherwise can last
for centuries. I walk to the door
with an uncovered window. Watch a crowd
of bees crawling up the other side
of the glass. Look through windows
not covered. Try to see
if there is a floor or only dirt.
I walk around the house on dry earth
and weeds so hard they push
up through my rubber soles.
A place to be now that love is gone.

According to the Hour

Years later, back on the island
in absolute light, I am trying
to remember what it was like.
There was seeing, then passion,
and then ravishment. After that
the punishment. It is important to me
that the world has not changed.
This morning the woman across the road
came out and pulled up an armload
of onions and went away.
The mountain of the gods is far
from town. The sea changes
its color according to the hour,
becoming palest just before dark.

"They Cripple with Beauty and Butcher with Love"

Eight years later the woman is given
a house for five months at the edge of town
in the desert. It's August and the desert is green.
When rain falls, she drives beyond the dark clouds.
Past an antelope, legs resting under it,
head raised, white marks. Drives slowly around
a turtle. If the man lied about love,
or even if it was true, there was immense damage.
When she woke, she was at the beginning where
love ends. Beauty everywhere on the road.
Silence inside her body in the clear
evening air, near the Mexican border.

Searching for the Poem

I.

The boat of the bible was
pushed into the reeds. Our chanting
is the stolen property of the sea.
Bathing is our clothing, is the mountain
I see in you. I walk up in the heat
to remember its weight. Which has
something to do with it. We are struck
dumb by what we call truth.
Having to match the foreignness of stone.
Our speech is far from the click
and shift of broken glass, making
the new colored pictures we try
to memorize in our sleep.
We are strengthened even by defeat,
honoring most what is strangest among us.

II.

I'm standing with a tree while
the sun rises, proud of the night.
She pushed the infant into the reeds
to keep the secret. Using language
for imitation. To keep the mountain
of the beloved. I walk up the mountain
in the heat to know belief. The glass
image shifts and clicks in our sleep.
Changes into another mystery
to turn the pages.

III.

The thing we are trying to say
is in the language of leaves.
We take our chanting from the sea
and clothe ourselves in the instruments
of water. We can never speak
its language. In the book they made
a boat of our reeds to hide
the child. We go down and forth,
proud to live with the night.
We walk up the mountain to relearn
the weight. To keep inside the beloved.
When we sleep the universe shifts
and clicks. We memorize each
new image and hide it for safety.
For our chanting. Get as close as possible
without knowing. Draw it with a stick.

THE STORIES ARE STRENUOUS

The story was about Orpheus getting
his head cut off by women
who had gathered under a tree.
How his head continued to sing.
When do we get to say that it's not true?
I saw him yesterday evening
walking through the village,
offending the neighborhood,
alarming the authorities. Breaking
the laws wholeheartedly
by the sweetness of his singing.

Bamboo and a Bird

In the subway late at night.
Waiting for the downtown train
at Forty-second Street.
Walking back and forth
on the platform.
Too tired to give money.
Staring at the magazine covers
in the kiosk. Someone passes me
from behind, wearing an orange vest
and dragging a black hose.
A car stops and the doors open.
All the faces are plain.
It makes me happy to be
among these people
who leave empty seats
between each other.

Always Alone

There was a place. It was not important.
A narrow street next to the sea in the town
where I waited for the bus to take me
back up to my house on top of the mountain.
I would buy a bottle of water and sit
on a step across from the wharf,
in the shade if I was lucky. I watched
the beaten-up fishing boats tied to the pier.
The fishermen sold their catch alongside.
Or sat idle on the decks, sometimes cooking
on small grills. Mostly I looked away,
to another mountain where I felt
the goddess used to be. Where I walked
so often in her absence. Finding
ancient shards, negotiating for my soul
with the leftover facts of the Earth.
Reconciling with what love is. Always alone.
Usually it was evening and I would be tired.
I would watch the boats, hear the Aegean,
consider the mountain that I had been intimate with.
Sometimes I would take a fragment
from my bag and spit on it. Or splash
on the last of my drinking water to see
if anything was there. Maybe a piece
of the classical black glaze
or the shadow of a flower. Maybe even
part of a maiden. In the pleasure
of the whole thing. Still a secret.

The Test Is Whether Anything Breaks Off When You Roll It Down Stairs

A dress hangs on the far wall
of a doorless room. Hot dry air,
hot dry light. The house has only
framing boards for a roof. A bathtub
sits alone outside. The stillness
eating the absence. A stuffed couch
and train tracks beyond. What's gone
makes what's left silent. The clatter,
roar and screams of the train
disappear into the hush.

QUIETLY

Now there is neither Hart Crane's "The dice of drowned
men's bones," or Blake's orchestra of angels.
Here bells are ringing, roosters crowing
and the doves' wings flapping. All sounds
are of faith in the graveyard behind this church
that slopes steeply down toward the far sea.
Some coffins have photographs on them.
Some with housed candles. Dry earth
and pine trees. The way David Park
would paint a few figures standing in the sea.
Quiet. In the moment. Outside the self
but near. Not knowing them. Painting them
simply. Red mark for a mouth, or blue
for the sea. Like the woman in the graveyard,
alone, turning left toward her dead son.
Replacing the old flowers with the new.
Late in June, nearly nine o'clock in the evening
where it is still light.

NOT KNOWING THE RULES

The two white-bellied antelope stood still
as I approached on the farm road at evening,
and three birds flew away. The air was clear
the way it is on the desert after rain,
the sky bright. I was wondering why,
besides the beauty, I was there. And how close
I felt to death. Waiting for the heart
to revive. Between objects and desire.
I waded on through the brilliant light
that comes here just before dark. Shining
on the grass in front of me from the back.

I Do Not Need the Gods to Return

I do not need the gods to return. I have
seen the fragments. Have weighed them
in my hand, one at a time in the heat.
One at a time, in the dry dirt. Oregano,
sage and thyme. I don't need Orpheus
to sing. I walk down the esplanade at night.
I pass one loud bar after the other.
On the left the sea, bigger and stronger
after dark. Orpheus put down his lyre
centuries ago. Who knows what the women
believe now that they are not guarded.
Who can tell if it is easier now. The wide fig
trees shade me either way. It has been
suggested that we should go back to the source.
The rain and fire that gave birth to all
of it. The paintings on jars. Burnt things.
And Aphrodite so much like a queen.
The cracking of almonds, the plowing
of the fields. The broken libation cup unbroken.
I don't need the old gods to be believed.
No Orpheus to sing again.

NOW I UNDERSTAND

Something was pouring out. Filling the field
and making it vacant. A wind blowing them
sideways as they moved forward. The crying
as before. Suddenly I understood why they left
the empty bowls on the table, in the empty hut
overlooking the sea. And knew the meaning
of the heron breaking branches, spreading
his wings in order to rise up out of the dark
woods into the night sky. I understood about
the lovers and the river in January.
Heard the crying out as a battlement,
of greatness, and then the dying began.
The height of passion. Saw the breaking
of the moon and the shattering of the sun.
Believed in the miracle because of the half heard
and the other half seen. How they ranged
and how they fed. Let loose their cries.
One could call it the agony in the garden,
or the paradise, depending on whether
the joy was at the beginning, or after.

The Singers Change, the Music Goes On

No one really dies in the myths.
No world is lost in the stories.
Everything is lost in the retelling,
in being wondered at. We grow up
and grow old in our land of grass
and blood moons, birth and goneness.
We live our myth in the recurrence,
pretending we will return another day.
Like the morning coming every morning.
The truth is we come back as a choir.
Otherwise Eurydice would be forever
in the dark. Our singing brings her
back. Our dying keeps her alive.

It Goes Away

I give everything away and it goes away,
into the dusty air,
onto the face of the water
that goes away beyond our seeing.
I give everything away
that has been given to me:
the voices of children under clouds,
the men in the parks at the chess tables,
the women entering and leaving bakeries.
God who came here by rock, by tree, by bird.
All things silent in my seeing.
All things believable in their leaving.
Everything I have I give away
and it goes away.

WHOEVER

You are not even dead yet.
I saw you again this morning
in Penn Station. In your disguise.
Small, thin, elderly. Dressed
haphazardly in unbuttoned layers.
With the cane, cap and scarf.
Unloved, but not as invisible
as you want. I don't know what to feel.
I am glad to see you sometimes.
I think there is a tenderness
in you. Like the way a bird flies.
Other times I think it is to keep
people away. Always it is unrehearsed
need. A fist of need. Never having
food set before you.

Highway 90

An owl lands on the side
of the road. Turns its head
to look at me going fast,
window open to the night
on the desert. Clean air,
and the great stars.
I'm trying to decide
if this is what I want.

New Poems

IF WE ARE QUIET

for Liam Rector (1949–2007)

Now that you are dead
I want to remember the year,
the month, the hour, and the season
when I began to write poetry.
A girl in the month of summer
in a downstairs room
of an empty house.
A window open.
I could hear the shallow creek
through the trees.
Now that you are dead
I want to leave this place,
this city summer with the window open
feeling the air touch my arm, my face.
And remember the hour
when I began to touch mystery
with the words in my head.
Now that you have shot yourself
I am leaning in the direction
of going back in my imagination
to the place where the fish swim,
bay balls, flowering buckeye tree.
Where what was secret was visible.
Something you could share with them.
The wall paintings of Thera.
Swallows flying over stones
and irises. A naked boy with a bowl.

And all the cracked white plaster
behind each image
to suggest that we are in the world.
Now that you are dead.
Now that you have shot yourself in the head
I want to go home
to the place of clean air.
I am tired of the theatre of death
when it is not true.
Your hand, your lost face, is still here.
I want to go to where what I know
is believed. To the behavior of the world
if we are quiet enough to see.

ANOTHER MOUNTAIN

1.

The quarry.
Winding dirt road.
Garbage dump. Sometimes
smoldering. A mountain
cut in half.

2.

Another mountain
with its view straight down
into a green gorge.
Then the sea.
No people.
No animals. No snakes. No mythology.

3.

Sparrows fly. Pigeons walk and fly.
Rock doves walk and fly.
A larger bird, blue with white
on the edge of its wings arrives.
A foreigner. I watch it wait on
a fence. Then fly. Blue jays
fly. A bird lies on a grassy
hill with its wings open, drying
them in the morning sun.
Then flies. A woodpecker makes
a knocking noise on the trunk
of a dying tree. Then flies.

4.

Fumbled with my fingers among
the stones near and in the creek.
The water smelled of what? Tannin?
Is that it? Dead leaves? And
clean, clear, moving water.
Feeling for the soft stones
we call soap stones the
Indians flattened and circled
as wampum. We found them.
Rubbed them against harder stone.
For many days and years this is
one of the things we did in the woods.

5.

The husband's death makes him larger
than in his life. Not himself
but the realm he lived in.
The other man went away
about the same time.
The calls I made went unanswered.
I am listening to the sound
the city makes all night.
Like granite remaking itself.
Feel at home equally in life, art,
and death. Each step.

6.

Blond and green. Shooting arrows into
bales of hay. Carrying hazelnuts
in a leather pouch on my belt.
Taking the gray, fuzzy, husks off
after picking them in the woods
on horseback. Gathering acorns.
Shelling them. Leaching them
in the creek. Then grinding them into mash
on a matate. Under bay trees.
The smell of ground under redwood
trees. The smell of ground
under fir trees. Watching red-tailed
hawks circle for hours. Years. Days.
The noble company I met after I left home.
Poetry. Their deaths.

7.

The crack of manzanita. Then soft air
under fir trees. Years later the Aegean and
night. The standards are as high as
Cimabue. Perhaps, finally, one must
find a home. Or not. Water the geranium
in the morning. Look out at Naxos over
the water. The sea is the between.
The distance known. Mapped. Written.

August in the East Village

Across the courtyard the painter
is making love to a young man.
On a bed near the screen window.
I see the double arms and
the younger man's t-shirt raised
to under his arms. The weather
is unusually pleasant this morning,
especially for August in New York City.
Now the naked man on top
is holding the boy, slipping his hands
under the few inches of white.
And the boy's hand lays gently
on the other's side. Then
they roll over and continue.
The visitor has bound his hair
in a band. There is kissing.
There is a cloth he pulls over
both of them.
The cool air hardly moves
the tree's bright leaves.
They are waving
without the morning light
leaving them.

BEING ELEVEN

Ruined by the loss of the secret house
away from our lives.
The innerness that can not be shared
except for poetry.
An embarrassment to tell
about a law removed from
the order of things.
A glance to the left is illegal,
a reason to lie or half lie.
Nothing will change the rules.
Our lives support
the culture and the history,
right and wrong.
Yearning for the fort in the woods.
The creek where you might
invent a plan
to make money at eleven
by riding a horse up the mountain.
Filling gunny sacks with loam
from under a tall fir tree
to sell to the neighbors on horseback.
A risk of invention in the stream of things.
My grown-up friend afraid of discovery.
To enter the realm of the private.
To drink tea with me and listen
to Akhmatova in Russian.
The weight and rhythm
of her serious voice.
The world of secrecy. Of loss.

The Generosity of Engagement

In the beginning the memory
turned loose in the now turned loose
in the memory of the word winnowing,
winnowed, that I believe in, believe in
in the long going summer of my remembrance
remembering. A faith in the flowers, a faith
in the chosen masters of saving
what to keep and what to throw away.
I learned what to say, hidden and saved.
My recumbent lesson of what is long lost
and saved. The magical unity made
out of what is holy, happy, and clean made.
Blessed by the occasion of my being.
Holy, holy, holy. Saved, saved, saved
in the memory under the turning over of
all things turned under, turned under, under.
Me being jerked away. A pleasing thing
on the strip of wet sand, pausing or walking
or dancing or what the world that hour said.
The generosity of engagement of the ecstatic
in the quiet normal over and over again.
Tidal in the hurry of the last hour.
Each day jerked, junked from the folds originally.
Then torn away a different time
because of the difficulty of the accomplishment.
Of the way so cleanly served, seen, or heard about
later by others in a den a different mauling.
The danger the waves might make.
I never endangered myself in the ocean waves

but was unguarded when people came.

Now the beginning of memory.

The cawing of gulls outcalling the calling of men.

Covering the quiet within.

LOSING THEM

Listening to Akhmatova tonight,
her poems and her life.
Her voice sounding
like a heavy ship on a heavier sea,
remembering Joseph Brodsky,
hands in his pockets, looking straight up,
reading his poems by heart. Poems
she helped give birth to. And his fierce
loyalty to the Russian art.
I see him now as if he were alive,
full of criticism, humor and respect.
Saying first, "You don't understand.
Always in water over your head."
Then, "Kisses." Finally a salute
at the airplane entry for the last time.

Hearing the Gods

I am content to live in silence
with the dead.
The company of here swept clean.
Where the dead and I use memory
to see the pomegranate tree
in Aegean morning light.
Or hear the sea familiar to the
underworld. Or trade a last kiss
for an unpicked flower. Or pat the earth
and see small dust rise. Or walk
quietly up a pathless hill there
and not there. There and given.
Hearing the speaking of the gods
in the sound of a grasshopper.
Hearing the sliding of the dead
in a lizard's tail. This week.
That summer. Here, there.

Behave Yourself

In 1968, the island of Rhodes.
In the village of Lindos, a girl came. I don't
remember her language, maybe German.
She was young, and slim, and beautiful.
But that is not what distinguished her.
Drove the men crazy so that
they couldn't do anything without
looking at her. What made her great
was her silence. She never spoke
to anyone. When she danced
she danced alone.
It was the time of the dictators
and I remember having to be
photographed by the police, the man
saying firmly, "Behave yourself."
A military man desired her
and when she did not respond
he and his friends went into her
house and found a small stash.
They sent her to a prison island.
We sailed to that place
with gifts for her. Toilet paper,
kotex, crayons, paper, maybe soap
even though none of us knew her.

ARRIVING

What do they say about the land of the dead?
About the ceremony of the body?
About women in long dresses?
What do they say about the innocence of the flesh?
What about the endeavor in nature
at ease with the dance and music?
Long ago beyond graves are worlds in state.
The cities still there in ruin. The neck of the ibex.
Walled gardens surrounded by desert.
Imagined lions guarding the gate.
All as it was before.
Worlds out of time still exist.
Worlds of achievement out of mind and remembering
just as the poem lasts.
In the concert of being present.
I have lost my lover and my youth.
I want to praise the meadow, the horse
rolling over in the river with me
as a girl underneath it. Surviving to see
the ferns in the woods, sunlight on blond hills.
And the aged apple trees
in a valley where there used to be a cabin.
Where someone lived. And where small inedible apples
grow. That the deer will eat.

You Never Loved Me

Barry came to my apartment from Greece.
Sat next to me at the round table.
Looked across the table at my other friend.
We knew this man for thirty-eight years.
He yelled at Jack for six hours.
"You never loved me. You love no one.
Your poems never loved anyone.
You do not grow. You are antique."
The expatriate from Greece.
We knew him in Lindos when he was
twenty-five. He left at four a.m. Jack
had sat up all night across the table
in a chair. His eyes were open all the time.
Near the beginning, he made his hands
into soft fists and banged on the table.
I knew these men all those years.
Barry would come down to the house
and Jack would get on the back of his
motorcycle and they'd go away.
Jack would return for dinner.
What they did was never told
except by rumor.
Maybe a naked woman on a roof.
Something like that. Now two things:
this meeting and me thinking
that every day I was alone,
was feeling empty, was washing the floor
with a bucket of water and a short broom.

Oil light, me swimming in the sea,
walking from first light until
an hour before dark. Stopping
to paint the color of the sea.

A Little Less Pleasing

Hell is just a little different from the world.
A little less rational. A little less pleasing.
Women gathering water. Still moving
in the usual way, making the same gestures.
Dark birds pecking and gouging
are behaving in the usual way only this time
the people keep screaming.
Heaven is the same. Fields without blame,
a single season. The same wheat and flowers.
The same sweet air we breathe each spring day.
And yet Eurydice stayed inside herself, passive.
Almost indifferent to where she lived.
Relinquishing her power as energy, her beauty
which worked fine in a field of flowers.
Which worked well with her parents and new husband,
and served her well being taken by this man.
Then that man. That world. Then the walk
with the guide whose name she was never told.
Or did not remember. To see vaguely the back
of a man walking twice as fast as she was going
while she was being led on a path upwards.
All arguments happened in the large room
while she was sequestered in one of the smaller rooms
off a long hall with a single bed and a stuffed doll.
Like the rooms of the whores I saw in Surabaya.
The girls holding my hands, smiling, giving me
a chair to sit with them in the window.

Captured

Namesake, shepherd, young man, kid.
Sitting on a table at the back of the taverna.
Dry wood, clean air. Drinking the free drinks
given to him by the fishermen
because he lived alone on the mountains.
Quiet and stars.
Because he returned with his flock once
a year. A simple thing
to be a myth to your people. The boy
looked down the whole evening.
The young had gone to Athens
to learn how to make money and have fun.
Each drink they gave him came with
a few almonds and a piece of bread
or a few olives and a piece of feta.
The road looked across at Thessaloniki.
The sea with the Turkish ships and the near war again.
The young man who lived alone
on the mountains with his sheep.

Never So Far

"the dead have enough poppies"

Marina Tsvetaeva

And the loving that unfolds
is the unseen
in this world of things.
Like the time of day, water in a well,
snakes on the road. Being alone
is the realm you mate with,
and the loneliness strangely ends
although you have never been so far
from home.

No One Listens

For fifty years, one passion.
Bought wherever love was sold.
A turn, a glance.
The water-spider glides on it.
Under, small fish.
Above, the scent of
bay trees rustling.
The un-famous.
She is led,
allows it out of tradition.
Carrying the vision
in her heart.
A turn, a glance that no one buys.
Below, sleeping shepherds.
Above, the naked feet.
The hem of his dress.
"Lead me to paradise" is
the refrain she sings.
Dumps a bucket of water
on the cement. Sweeps with
a Greek broom. No one
arrives for all the years
to step on the drying floor.
The door open.

I Wish I Could Believe

I wish I could believe that the dead speak,
first to each other, and then
balanced between the here and the better
beyond, loitering for a while
to look at their stabbed and bloodied bodies.
To move forward through time
to that better place.
I wish I could believe
in the paper money
laid on the graves once a year.
And the cooked chicken with its feet
cut off on the graves
before sunrise when the dead
have to go home
above the tropical trees away from our
arriving light outside the village
in the mountains of Batu.
I wish I could believe
the way the youngest daughter
of the Atmajya family
did when she stood next to me
in front of the restaurant, looking at
the bull made out of four boys,
a handmade head
and a cloth over them. I asked her,
what does this mean?
And she said, one by one the boys
will become delirious and fall on the street.
The old men will rush up

and put a stick in his mouth sideways.
And carry him off the street as evidence
of a god's possession.
I wish I believed.
I sort of believed in something. In every sacred
thing. In drunkenness,
in desire, in the body's
physical transformations.
Depending on how many parts were
present at the occasion of the rebirth.
The soul barks, the soul meows.
The spirit tries to remember the words
that it is trying to sing.
The mind remembers beautiful things.
For me it was the scent of Herba Buena.
Such flimsy representations
of the crossover of things.
What comes here to awaken us.
But I believe it could be anything.
Some crazy woman in the subway
could be the chance
to be reconciled to the shapeliness
of one's own being.
Could be, could be. Or even
using memory
with eyes closed
feeling the weight
of a ripe pomegranate
and know
what it is.

GETTING DOWN

The snake leads the way
to a place of absolutes
where no man can talk
you out of anything.
It's a place as real as
an empty pool in front
of the not-in-service-at-
this-time motel. Each
person has a secret world.
Places where nobody can
visit. Places we live in
after our death.
The temple on the hill
is abandoned. There's no one
even to light its lamp unless
I do it. Afterward, I fall
asleep on the warm stones.
Safe. In my dream I realize
the truth about Orpheus.
He never went far into
the dark before turning around.

JUST BEFORE NIGHT

That evening. That darkening.
When the fishermen run
down the docks and jump
on the boats already leaving,
lights on the front facing down
into the Aegean all night.

THE RICHNESS OF LOSS

It has happened now. Not death but the time
of no horses, no acropolis.
Not a time of doubt, but of lessening.
November fields bare of cattle.
Statues without faces. The time after
moving into emptiness.
Housed in the abandoned being,
warehoused in spirit. Like the child
standing up in the backseat
looking at the house she knew
receding. Getting smaller and smaller.
On the Fourth of July I waited
with my sister all day
for it to get dark. Then each
was given one sparkler.
We lit it with a wooden kitchen match
and stood still on the wide dirt
looking at the flower it made,
the one we blew without knowing
its name was dandelion.
We ran silently in a circle
seeing each other's face
in the special light.
Then it was dark again.
Mountains all around, the smell it made
and the stars above our heads.

Walking on the Bottom of the World

An absolute can be made of what
is missing, of disappeared love
frozen in memory of the sky
over a city I lived in. But the world
cannot resist being rich. I walk
on desert road 2810 at evening
and the whole begins to break apart.
Into life, history and a fence.
I return toward the setting sun,
swimming in a universe of light.
Walking on this ancient land
that used to be the floor of an ocean.

THE SOURCE OF ROMANTIC LOVE

Ishi came out of hiding
after his sister died. (The last of his tribe.)
His brain is now in Washington, a number.
His heart buried. Air over the Aegean.
Nine months of an almond tree.
The goat. The old woman shivering,
rocking on the bench in front of her house.
Old husband riding on a donkey to the taverna.
Hot water bottle for her. A baby goat.
And later Hagia Sophia, doors the depth
of a soldier's step. Shone on by sunlight
off the gold mosaics surrounding an image
of Christ. A glass of pomegranate juice.

CHRIST LOVED BEING HOUSED

The time of passion is younger than us.
It does not live in memories
or metaphors, but in living things:
quail, bay trees, the sun leaving
and returning. Going and being there.
Dark, rain, and colors spreading
through the late sky afterward.
So much like the Apache and Tarahumara
who live differently now, as I do.
But I want to ask you about the nature
of love. Do you think it is unearthly?
I want to tell you it is, and more.
Christ did not want to leave the body.
Love resides entirely in the part of us
that is the least defended or safe.
The part that has no alternative
to loss, defeat, and dying.
All else is tested by its flint
in what it strikes upon in the darkness.

Stopping

Leaning against huge boulders
with the sea at our backs
waiting for the Greek bus near dark.
Then on the bus looking out
at the night.
The outskirts in the mountains.
Walking up the street made of
stone. Stopping
to buy tomatoes and ice cream
while Jack stands outside
looking at the adults sitting
and children playing in the small
town square. When I came back,
he had figured out the game.
One child is riding a bicycle
around the fountain. Another
running behind with her arms out
pretending. After that
the narrow streets.
Stopping to see the pomegranate.
To look at the moon.
Naxos from my patio and the
moon. Before entering the house.

Acknowledgments

I wish to thank Peter Weltner, Bob Stephens, and Donald Brees.

"'Wherefore Dost Bruise Me?' He Exclaimed, Weeping,
and Like a Corpse Fell to the Ground" is for Timothy Liu.

The Greensboro Review: "Arriving"
Waccamaw: "Just Before Night"

LINDA GREGG (1942–2019) was the author of six books of poetry: *Too Bright to See*, *Alma*, *The Sacraments of Desire*, *Chosen by the Lion*, *Things and Flesh*, and *In the Middle Distance*. *All of It Singing: New and Selected Poems* won the Lenore Marshall Poetry Prize from the Academy of American Poets, the William Carlos Williams Award from the Poetry Society of America, and the American Book Award from the Before Columbus Foundation. She received the PEN/Voelcker Award in Poetry for achievement across her career, the Jackson Poetry Prize from Poets & Writers, and had received a Whiting Award and fellowships from the Guggenheim Foundation, the Lannan Foundation, and the National Endowment for the Arts. Born in New York and raised in Marin County, California, Gregg served as a beloved teacher at many colleges and universities, and died in 2019 in New York City.

The text of *All of It Singing* has been set in Adobe Garamond Pro, drawn by Robert Slimbach and based on type cut by Claude Garamond in the sixteenth century. This book was designed by Ann Sudmeier. Composition by BookMobile Design and Publishing Services, Minneapolis, Minnesota. Manufactured by Versa Press on acid-free 30 percent postconsumer wastepaper.

This book is made possible through a partnership with the College of Saint Benedict, and honors the legacy of S. Mariella Gable, a distinguished teacher at the College.

Previous titles in this series include:

Loverboy by Victoria Redel
The House on Eccles Road by Judith Kitchen
One Vacant Chair by Joe Coomer
The Weatherman by Clint McCown
Collected Poems by Jane Kenyon
Variations on the Theme of an African Dictatorship
  by Nuruddin Farah:
       Sweet and Sour Milk
       Sardines
       Close Sesame
Duende by Tracy K. Smith
The Art of Syntax: Rhythm of Thought, Rhythm of Song
  by Ellen Bryant Voigt
How to Escape a Leper Colony by Tiphanie Yanique

Support for this series has been provided by the Lee and Rose Warner Foundation as part of the Warner Reading Program.